# 12 SIMPLE SECRETS

## *of* HAPPINESS

## AT WORK

---

FINDING

FULFILLMENT,

REAPING

REWARDS

---

Glenn Van Ekeren

Foreword by Bestselling Author Zig Ziglar

Prentice
Hall Press

**Library of Congress Cataloging-in-Publication Data**

Van Ekeren, Glenn.
  12 simple secrets of happiness at work / Glenn Van Ekeren.
      p. cm.
    ISBN 0-7352-0255-9 (pbk.)
    1. Job satisfaction.   2. Self-realization.   3. Interpersonal relations.
4. Happiness.   I. Title: Twelve simple secrets of happiness at work.
II. Title.
HF5549.5.J63 V36 2001
650.14—dc21                                         00-068480
                                                    CIP

*Acquisitions Editor: Tom Power*
*Senior Production Editor: Jackie Roulette*
*Formatter: Amy Koval*
*Designer: Sue Behnke*

© *2001 by Glenn Van Ekeren*

*Printed in the United States of America*

*10 9 8 7 6 5 4 3*

ISBN   0-7352-0255-9   (p)

**ATTENTION: CORPORATIONS AND SCHOOLS**

Prentice Hall Press books are available at quantity discounts with bulk purchase for educational, business, or sales promotional use. For information, please write to: Prentice Hall Special Sales, 240 Frisch Court, Paramus, New Jersey 07652. Please supply: title of book, ISBN, quantity, how the book will be used, date needed.

Paramus, NJ 07652

http://www.phdirect.com

# CONTENTS

ACKNOWLEDGMENTS

*I want to thank my parents who taught me the value of work at an early age, provided the example of a good work ethic, and encouraged me to give my best at whatever I did.*

*Thank you to my wife, Marty, and my children, Matt and Katy, for helping me to keep my work in perspective. You are the joy of my life.*

*Thank you to the crew at Prentice Hall Press for continuing to turn my writing dreams into reality.*

When I saw the title, *Twelve Simple Secrets of Happiness at Work*, I was reminded of a quote my friend Dr. Steve Franklin, formerly of Emory University, made several years ago. This translation is undoubtedly by now a paraphrase, but the message is clear: The greatest truths in life are the simple ones. You don't need four moving parts and five syllables for something to be profound. There are actually only three pure colors in existence, but look what Michelangelo did with those three colors. There are only ten mathematical digits, but look what Einstein did with them. There are only seven musical notes, but Chopin, Beethoven, and Vivaldi created masterpieces with them. To this I often add, look what Elvis did with just two!

The message in *Twelve Simple Secrets of Happiness at Work* is profound. Glenn Van Ekeren has called upon the wisdom that's been generated over centuries by outstanding people from every walk of life. In his research (which was extensive) Glenn quotes many of my own favorite sources and brings everything together, i.e., whatever the problem, there is a solution—and it is often a simple one. He emphasizes that when you strive to be your best, work at it with passion, accept responsibility for who you are, what you do, and what happens—it covers the critical areas of life.

Glenn is an enjoyable author to read. He brings out the good, gently chastises that which is not so good, then offers a better, simpler way of accomplishing what needs to be done. In the process, he deals with virtually every facet of life—team play, love, process, looking for the good and opportunity in each situation that life brings. In the process, he teaches us that the only way to coast is downhill and that we should have structure to whatever we do but still be willing to get "outside the box."

The neat thing about this book is that it's one that can be shared with every member of the family and with others, regardless of occupation or goals in life. This book will enable readers to be more loving at home, more effective at work, and better citizens in the community.

*Zig Ziglar, author and motivational teacher*

I've worked a variety of jobs in my lifetime. As I made my way through high school and college, I did everything from laying sod balls to lugging steel to being an ecology specialist (garbage hauler) to washing dishes in the college cafeteria to working as a camp counselor, which allowed me to sleep in a tent for ten weeks one summer. These less-than-glamorous jobs involved a lot of mundane tasks and got downright boring at times. I often marveled at the work I was willing to do just to make some money when the paycheck often seemed like a minor reward.

Most of us have endured such work experiences and learned at an early age that every job seemed to require doing a lot of things we didn't like to do. Daydreaming often became my escape from those small, dull, routine jobs. Although I loved to dream about achieving some exciting career, my real–world experiences got me to thinking that any career I chose in the future would probably require me to perform less–than–desirable tasks…And I was right.

The challenge was to concentrate and focus my energies on the things I liked to do. This simple discovery transformed the way I approach work and paved the way for experiencing 25 years of work fulfillment and career satisfaction. IBM executive Buck Rogers once said, "Our work has to be more than an unfortunate necessity, an unpleasant means of paying the bills. We owe it to ourselves and to the people who are important to us to demand more out of all those hours. It's our responsibility to make sure our work gives us the pleasure of pride, accomplishment, and congenial relationships."

People who expect their work to totally fulfill them, their salary to always be what they want it to be, and their career to include only things they enjoy doing are going to be gravely disappointed. It is our responsibility to make our career more than just a means of making a living. Your job can be wonderful or miserable. The difference depends on you.

The *12 Simple Secrets of Happiness at Work* takes a refreshing look at what work can be and is helpful in rethinking our approach to work. The revitalizing principles fall into one of the following three important factors: ability, attitudes, and behavior. Of the thousands of jobs available in the marketplace, I can't think of one where these three factors don't have an influence.

**Ability.** Calvin Coolidge noted: "Few people are lacking in capacity, but they fail because they are lacking in application." W.C. Fields amassed considerable wealth during his lifetime. He attempted to keep it a secret by tucking money away in an estimated 200 bank accounts throughout the United States and Europe. The accounts were opened under an assumed name. At the time of his death, the executors of his estate located only 45 of the accounts. An estimated $600,000 remain uncovered. Imagine what those untapped assets would be worth today.

Many people possess latent abilities and unused talents. Unused talents may soon become rusty, antiquated, or even misplaced and lost forever. One of the marvelous natural laws of life is that when we invest ourselves through the use of talents and abilities, that which we invest will be multiplied. Using our abilities to the fullest will expand those talents and produce additional opportunities to use them.

**Attitude.** We can choose one of two attitudes toward our career. The first is characterized by Thomas Edison's view of work: "I never did a day's work in my life. It was all fun." Edison believed the purpose of work was productivity, joy, and fulfillment. Most of what we know about Edison reveals he was a living example of his work beliefs.

King Sisyphus, an evil king in Greek mythology, exemplified a totally different attitude. Sisyphus was condemned to Hades for eternity. His daily duty was pushing a large rock up a mountain, which at the end of the day, rolled down again. Each day was a repeat of the last, filled with drudgery, monotony, and a meaningless end result. Hordes of people view their daily responsibilities as replicating the uninspired, fruitless experience of King Sisyphus.

B.C. Forbes wrote, "Whether we find pleasure in our work or whether we find it a bore depends entirely on our mental attitude toward it, not on the task itself." The secret to happiness, success, satisfaction, and fulfillment in our work is not doing what one likes, but in liking what one does. It's an individual choice. "Fall in love with what you are going to do for a living," said George Burns. "I'd rather be a failure in something that I love than be successful in something that I hate."

Just remember, a side benefit to Thomas Edison's approach is that if you love what you do, you'll never have to work another day in your life.

**Behaviors.** Industrialist Andrew Carnegie said, "The average person puts only 25 percent of their (sic) energy and ability into their (sic) work. The world takes off its hat to those who put in more than 50 percent of their capacity, and stands on its head for those few-and-far-between souls who devote 100 percent."

I've had the opportunity to help friends move to different homes. You can learn a lot about your friends when there is physical labor to be performed. I often noticed when there is a piano to be moved, there is always someone volunteering to carry the bench. Have you ever noticed how many people are like that at work? They willingly volunteer to do the things they enjoy or the easy tasks; but when it comes to tackling the undesirable jobs, they are nowhere to be found.

It's impressive to watch some people, no matter what their position, pitch in and do the things others don't like to do. They are paving the way for elevated work excitement by investing themselves in results, serving others and the common good. They have learned the amazing degree of satisfaction that can be experienced by volunteering to do what other people avoid and doing it better than anyone else thought possible. Martin Luther King, Jr. said, "If you are called to be a street sweeper, sweep streets even as Michelangelo painted, or Beethoven composed music, or Shakespeare wrote poetry.

Sweep streets so well that all the host of heaven and earth will pause to say, 'here lived a great street sweeper who did his job well.'"

In the work world, there is a fair amount of people standing on the sidelines preparing to get in the game. They will jump in when the "just right" position comes along. They'll volunteer to give a little more of themselves when the money is just right. They go above and beyond the call of duty when they are assured their efforts will be noticed. The game clock keeps ticking and they keep waiting. It's too bad, but some never get into the game.

Chuck Colson, writing in *Why America Doesn't Work,* observed, "No matter how many structures we fix, no matter how many laws we reform, restoring the work ethic in our society ultimately boils down to one thing; we must restore it in the hearts and minds of individuals." The success of any office, production crew, sales force, or service provider is dependent on the individual investment of people in what they do. Nothing succeeds until people make it happen.

Whatever your chosen career, get into it. Stop looking at work as simply a means of making a living or the price you pay to climb a corporate ladder. Understand that work is an essential ingredient in making a quality life. When you drench yourself in what you do, the rewards will follow.

The self-esteem, satisfaction, and fulfillment you experience at work depends on you. To transform your daily "have-to's" into a lifestyle of "want-to's," consider these two questions: "What do I want out of my life's work?" and "What am I willing to do to make it happen?" *12 Simple Secrets of Happiness at Work* contains the resources necessary for you to get into the game and enjoy the contribution you can make.

12 SIMPLE SECRETS *of* HAPPINESS AT WORK

# INFUSE YOUR
# WORK WITH
# PASSION

❄

*Motivation is a fire from within. If someone
else tries to light that fire under you,
chances are it will burn briefly.*

STEPHEN COVEY

## LIGHT YOURSELF
## ON FIRE

"Once upon a time there was a guy named Joe who had a very lousy job." Those are the opening words of Stephen Spielberg's 1990 movie, *Joe Versus the Volcano.*

In the movie, Joe Banks (Tom Hanks) reaches a point of total frustration with his job and his life. Everyday is bad Monday. His boss is always in a bad mood. The cumulative stresses convince Joe his energy-stripped life is irreparable. Exasperated and depressed, he laments, "I'm losing my soul." Soon after Joe learns he is plagued with terminal "brain cloud" (a fictitious diagnosis that convinced Joe he was mentally asleep).

Unemployed and desperate, Joe coincidentally encounters an eccentric jillionaire (played by Lloyd Bridges) who presents a proposition that allows Joe to turn his mediocre, dead-end, unfulfilled life around. All he must do in return is

*Success is not the result of spontaneous combustion. You must set yourself on fire.*

REGGIE LEACH

journey to the island of Waponi Woo and leap into a volcano. Joe leaps at the chance.

Aboard the jillionaire's yacht, Joe meets Patricia, one of the wealthy man's daughters. In awe of the incredible turn of events and the new life he has enjoyed since meeting her father, Joe looks into the moonless, star-filled night and exclaims, "Your life is unbelievable—just unbelieveable!"

Patricia's response was profound. "My father says that almost the whole world is asleep—everybody you know, everybody you see, everybody you talk to. He says that only a few people are awake, and they live in a state of constant, total amazement."

The movie was a commercial disaster and a popular target of cynical movie critics who missed this scene, or at least misinterpreted Spielberg's attempt at jolting people into "waking up."

Paul Goodman, the famous linguist and social commentator, estimated that as many as 82 percent of American workers don't like being at work and can't wait to be freed from what work does to them. They are the Joe Bankses of the world who need an immediate wake-up call, preferably (for them) without the threat of terminal "brain cloud."

People who depend on others for the condition of their morale do themselves a huge disservice. No organization or supervisor can adequately be empowered to pump you up.

It's so popular today to plead victimization by the system, circumstances, competition, rightsizing, or other external factor. Human spirits are buffeted by increased pressures from co-workers, job demands, or the daily grind of everyday living. Indifference slithers in to replace motivation and a vicious cycle of unhappiness begins.

Blaming, finger-pointing, and accusing are popular anecdotes for attitudes gone sour. Steer free from such self-defeating behavior. Take charge of your moods. Fill your energy tank. Corral negative emotions. Bury grudges and perceived unfairness. Recognize your present mental attitudes about the job and get serious about an action plan to help you out of the ruts.

There is an old Texas saying that indicates "You can't light a fire with a wet match." What's your "flammable quotient"? Are your coals smoldering? Are the flames hot and high?

Are you alive with excitement about your work? Are you doing what you love? Light yourself on fire. Become a passionate, self-igniting morale arsonist rather than operating on the erroneous assumption that someone else will make your job more exciting or more challenging.

I often ask applicants what prompted them to apply at our organization. It never ceases to amaze me how many people respond, "I thought you might have a job I would like." Sorry. We don't have any jobs like that. However, we do have a lot of people who like their jobs.

Your job (no matter how great or lousy it is) can be more than a way to earn a living. Make it an important element in creating a quality life. You don't need to jump into a volcano to light yourself on fire. Reenergizing your work spirit is an inside job.

## THE MONEY
## IS THE GRAVY

Denis Waitley, in *Empires of the Mind,* shared the experience of attending his daughter's college graduation. Fearing the exercises would be long and merciless, Waitley was relieved when the keynote speaker took the podium. The speaker was Edward James Olmos, the actor–activist who played Jaime Escalante in an inspiring movie about inner-city students called *Stand and Deliver.*

According to Waitley, Olmos stood up, removed his cap, and regarded the graduates. "So we're ready to party?" he asked. "Yeah, let's party!" they answered in unison. "I know, thank God it's Friday," he resumed. "But commencement means to begin, not finish. You've had a four-year sabbatical from life, and now you're ready to go out there and earn. You're only beginning Real World 101 in your education.

"One more thing before we leave," he continued. "Please never, ever work for money. Please don't just get a job. A job is something that many of you had while you were working

*To fulfill a dream, to be allowed to sweat over lonely labor, to be given a chance to create, is the meat and potatoes of life. The money is the gravy.*

BETTE DAVIS
*The Lonely Life*

❋

your way through college. A job is something you do for money. But a career is something you do because you must do it. You want to do it, you love doing it, you're excited when you do it. And you'd do it even if you were paid nothing beyond food and basics. You do it because it's your life."

Rarely does our educational training prepare us to find a career that is satisfying. We go to college, learn skills, and then find a company that offers a paycheck in exchange for our knowledge and a few hours of work. If only we could inject every college graduate and potential employee with this admonishment, "Pursue a passion, not a paycheck." This simple insight could save a multitude of people from being disillusioned. Charles Schwab, steel magnate, concluded: "The man who does not work for the love of work but only for money is not likely to make money nor find much fun in life." No matter how little or how much your chosen career pays in money, if you pursue it with passion, you'll go to work every day with the satisfaction of knowing you are making a difference.

We all need the money. That is a given. But, work goes beyond what you do to earn a paycheck; it involves personal commitment, personal satisfaction, and personal growth. Like it or not, these results—along with promotions and pay increases—are rewards for achieving results, not just doing work. Results are realized when we apply and develop our strengths. In *Goodbye Job, Hello Me,* Wexler and Wolf suggest, "The fascination of simply making money wears thin in time. The real fruits of one's labors are seen in the planting of one's gifts." When you are involved in a company that shares your values and you are doing a job that utilizes your talents and skills, a meaningful career will blossom.

"Is my occupation what I get paid money for, or is it something larger and wider and richer—more a matter of what I am or how I think about myself," questioned Robert Fulghum. "Making a living and having a life are not the same thing. Making a living and making a life that's worthwhile are not the same thing. A job title doesn't even come close to answering the question, 'What do you do?' Possessing a title or allowing money to possess you does not answer the questions, "Who are you?" or "What do you do?"

People want jobs that matter. Tom Brokaw said, "It's easy to make a buck. It's a lot tougher to make a difference." What makes this difficult is that each of us must discover for ourselves what activities are meaningful and allow us the opportunity to make a difference. If you've been feeling disenfranchised, unmotivated, dissatisfied, or apathetic,

*First find
something you
like to do so
much you'd
gladly do it for
nothing; then
learn to do it so
well people are
happy to pay
you for it.*

WALT DISNEY

❁

there's a chance you've not yet realized that it takes more than money to light the fire of passion.

How many people do you know work in a job they dislike so they can earn enough money to do the things they like to do? What a dead-end, dissatisfying, unfulfilling way to approach a job.

Historically, people have viewed work as a required necessity to make a living, but actually living was reserved for after-hours. Times are changing. There's a visible epidemic among people questioning what they really want out of life and work. A paycheck and a few benefits are no longer sufficient to generate passion and achieve meaning.

Immerse yourself in whatever you are doing. Don't go to work because you have to. Go to work to make a difference. Instead of complaining that you can't find a job you like, concentrate on what you like about your job. Transform your thinking and design strategies to creatively enhance the contribution you make. View yourself as a little company inside of the larger one. Hold yourself accountable for the success of your department. You are the organization. What you do matters. And, remember "The money is the gravy."

## CONTENTMENT BREEDS DISCONTENTMENT

I t's dangerous to rest on our past successes. In the book *The Eighty-Yard Run,* a college freshman at his first football practice breaks loose for an 80-yard touchdown run. His teammates immediately place him in high esteem and the coach lets him know he will have quite a future with the team. His pretty blonde girlfriend picks him up after practice and awards him with a passionate kiss. He has the feeling his life is now set, his future secure.

*If I see myself today as I was in the past, my past must resurrect itself and become my future.*
WILLIAM JAMES

Unfortunately, nothing in his life ever matches that day again. His football experiences never rise above the level of mediocrity, nor does his business career. His marriage goes sour and the disappointment is even greater because he continually reflects back on that day of glory when he was convinced that life would always be pleasant and act favorably toward him.

This young man, and the rest of humankind for that matter, could learn something from the Wisconsin dairy industry. On the side of their milk bottles are printed these words: "Our cows are not contented. They're anxious to do better."

Contentment breeds discontentment. When you're satisfied with savoring the past, in lieu of creating your future, the present loses its appeal. Aspiring to excel, our last achievement inspires us to grow beyond the present. Continuing to think about the same things day after day or attempting to build our lives based on the past is anti-productive. Don't get me wrong, your past is important, but only to the degree your experiences inspire you to new levels of living. Life is more meaningful when you are searching for ways to exceed your past performance, not being content with it.

Johann Wolfgang von Goethe hit a nerve when he said, "Things that matter most must never be at the mercy of things that matter least." Contentment with your favorite foods, road to work, most watched television programs, most frequently worn outfit, and the like is just fine—although I would suggest a little variation to put some spice in your life. These are trivial issues compared to the performance practices, habits, attitudes, approach to problems, relation-ship skills, and other "most" items Goethe alluded to, that significantly affect your future success.

Many years ago, an aspiring Greek artist named Timanthes submitted himself to the instruction of a well-known tutor. Working diligently for several years, the young artist created a portrait that displayed the artistic talent he had developed. Thrilled with the outcome, Timanthes sat day after day gazing at his work.

Early one morning he arrived at the studio to discover his teacher had destroyed his masterpiece. Devastated, angry, and drowning in his tears, he begged an explanation from his tutor. The wise artist replied, "I did it for your own good. That painting was retarding your progress. It was an excellent piece of art, but it was not perfect. Start again and see if you can do even better."

Stunned, yet stimulated, Timanthes put his brush to the canvas and eventually produced a masterpiece called "Sacrifice of Iphigenia."

Fight hard to remain free of long-term contentment and satisfaction with your past accomplishments. Strive for higher plateaus. You'll never have to look back and wish you could go there. It's exciting to work and live with positive anticipation for what can happen next. As Disney's Pocahantas said, "You'll see things you never knew you never knew."

*Workers develop routines when they do the same job for a while. They lose their edge, falling into habits not just in what they do but in how they think. Habits turn into routines. Routines into ruts.*

ROBERT KRIEGEL

## THERE'S NO NEED TO BE MISERABLE

How happy are you with your job? Are there times when misery is more prevalent than happiness? Have you learned to be happy in spite of circumstances, job responsibilities, or people?

Norman Cousins, the late author and editor of *Saturday Review*, wrote, "Happiness is probably the easiest emotion to feel, the most elusive to create deliberately, and the most difficult to define. It is experienced differently by different people." Although happiness is different for each of us, here are a few generic principles worth thinking about.

**1. End the search.** People who place the search for happiness as the top priority in their life will struggle to experience it. "Happiness is a butterfly—the more you chase it, the more it flies away from you and hides," wrote Rabbi Harold Kushner in the best-selling book *When All You've Ever Wanted Isn't Enough*. "But stop chasing it, put away your net and busy yourself with other, more productive things than the pursuit of happiness, and it will sneak up on you from behind and perch on your shoulder."

**2. Evaluate your expectations.** Thinking you can be happy with your job all the time is an unrealistic expectation. It won't happen, no matter how hard you try, even if you read every word in this book and implement each suggestion. When you expect your job to make you happy, you've already put yourself in a disadvantageous position. Add to this a desperate pursuit of this elusive emotion and you'll understand why so many people are miserable in their job.

For the most part, I expect to enjoy a happy, satisfied, fulfilled career. But when it doesn't happen, a sense of misery and discontent settles in. Within moments, I'm acutely aware of how my expectations and reality are in conflict. It's a natural setup for disappointment. Author Max Lucado offers this valuable advice, "Remember, disappointment is caused by unmet expectations. Disappointment is cured by revamped expectations." It's a huge mistake to set our expectations so high that they are unattainable or depend on our work to be the sole source of happiness. The problem, of course, is that only rarely do our jobs, other people, or life in general live up to the expected ideal.

**3. Exit your misery.** Actor and singer Dean Martin died a few years ago. His closest friends commented upon his death that, although he had now died physically, Dean Martin had given up on life years earlier. After his son died in a plane crash, Martin was vocal about his loss of interest in living. Without his son, he no longer wanted to live himself and yearned to die. Friends tried to help him through these difficult times, but Martin was intent that life was over for him. He became a recluse, refused to see friends, and spent his days watching television by himself. His son's tragic death overwhelmed his desire to live.

It's a dangerous thing to hang our happiness on the shoulders of some other person, a career, or a business. As tragic as the event was, Dean Martin still had a lot of life to live. He could have toured with his good friend Frank Sinatra, relished the offers of dinner and enjoyed fellowship with close friends, or poured himself into a number of useful causes. Instead, he gave up on life. He is not alone in this response.

I certainly am not implying that our work compares in value to our relationships. Yet, when people die, life does go on. We grieve. We reflect. We cherish the good times. Expectations are adjusted. We go on. Likewise, we will experience disappointment, unmet expectations, and the death of dreams and goals in our work lives. We refocus, carefully monitoring our reactions, and push forward. It is simply a waste of time and talent to give up and give in to misery.

**4. Entertain an agenda other than your own.**
I received an article from an unknown source titled "How to Be Miserable." It says, "Think about yourself. Talk about yourself. Use `I' as often as possible. Mirror yourself continually in the opinion of others. Listen greedily to what people say about you. Expect to be appreciated. Be suspicious. Be jealous and envious. Be sensitive to slights. Never forgive a criticism. Trust nobody but yourself. Insist on consideration and respect. Demand agreement with your own views on everything. Sulk if people are not grateful to you for favors shown them. Never forget a service you have rendered. Shirk your duties if you can. Do as little as possible for others."

I often find the people most unhappy with their work are those who choose to constantly think about themselves and how unhappy they are. The happiest people I encounter are so busy creating and enjoying life, they don't even think about being happy. Their happiness is a by-product of the unselfish effort they put forth. Greta Palmer wisely observed, "Those only are happy who have their minds on some object other than their own happiness—on the happiness of others, on the improvement of mankind, even on some art or pursuit followed not as a means but as itself an ideal end."

**5. Expand your thinking.** Dale Carnegie suggested that, "Happiness doesn't depend upon who you are or what you have; it depends solely upon what you think." If you continually think about yourself—what you want, the desire for a more exciting job, dissatisfaction with your salary, the need for a vacation, a better boss, or simply for the sun to shine to brighten your spirits—then misery rather than happiness will remain your companion. Remove yourself from the temptation of sponsoring a personal pity party and do something about what you can do something about. Get on with it. You'll be amazed at how quickly your actions will modify your thinking and emotions.

**6. Energize the current situation.** Being happy in a job that isn't what you thought it would be—or should be— isn't easy. If you fall into the category of the people continually dissatisfied with their jobs, there is hope. You do have a choice to be happier on the job by focusing and acting on the influences within your control. You can also decide to remain forever miserable.

Charlie "Tremendous" Jones reminds us that, "If you can't be happy where you are, it's a cinch you can't be happy where you ain't." In other words, if you can't be happy now with what you have, with what you do and who you are, you will not be happy when you get what you think you want. Happiness comes with learning the skill of living each moment and making the best of it. Certain experiences, job tasks, and people might make it easier for us to be happy, but they do not have the power to make you happy unless you allow them to. You have a choice to be happy or unhappy with your circumstances. Because you are one or the other, why not choose happiness.

When unhappiness reveals its ugly head, remind yourself of the temporary nature of misery—if you choose it to be. Happiness won't resurrect itself if we sulk and brood about the fact that we aren't so happy as we think we should be or would like to be. "It's good to be just plain happy," suggests Henry Miller. "It's a little better to know that you're happy; but to understand that you're happy and to know why and how . . . and still be happy, be happy in the being and the knowing, well that is beyond happiness, that is bliss." Master this attitude and as you move forward in life, you'll notice that happiness follows you. Stop chasing happiness and allow it to catch up with you.

*To experience happiness, we must train ourselves to live in this moment, to savor it for what it is, not running ahead in anticipation of some future date nor lagging behind in the paralysis of the past.*
LUCI
SWINDOLL

❁

# GOOD ENOUGH
# NEVER IS

*Then let us all do what is right, strive with all our might toward the unattainable, develop as fully as we can the gifts God has given us, and never stop learning.*

LUDWIG VON BEETHOVEN

## LEARNERS WILL INHERIT
## THE FUTURE

I t's hard to believe, watching Peter Jennings on the "ABC Evening News," that he wasn't always a smooth anchorperson. His first experience, while in his twenties, did not establish him as an experienced, audience-friendly journalist.

*My job is so secret that even I don't know what I'm doing.*

WILLIAM WEBSTER

After three years in his anchor position, Jennings made a bold move. He quit his envious position reading the news and retreated into the trenches to refine his skills as a working reporter. In their informative book, *Anchors: Brokaw, Jennings, Rather and the Evening News,* Robert Goldberg and Gerald Jay Goldberg provide an insightful look at Jennings's journey to becoming a respected TV journalist. They describe how Jennings, who never finished college, used the road as his educational classroom. He covered a wide variety of stories in the United States, became the first network correspondent on permanent assignment in the Middle East, moved to London, and covered other cities in Europe before returning to the anchor slot at ABC.

To be successful in today's business environment, you would be wise to seek hands-on experiences, intellectual stimulation, and an appreciation for information that can boost your effectiveness. Climbing the career ladder or attaining a positive reputation in your current position is precipitated by the ability to learn, absorb, adapt, and apply information that keeps your skills on the cutting edge. You need to be accountable for continually auditing your skill level through self-reflection and pursuing opportunities that take your professionalism to the next level.

By reading, listening, taking risks, and gaining exposure to new experiences, you can overcome ignorance that breeds complacency and blocks career vitality. Professional competence requires a consistent updating of your skill portfolio and the ability to stimulate learning throughout your entire work life. Make your job your classroom. Your knowledge bank is valuable to the organization and keeps your skills from becoming outdated. When your job is flowing smoothly, double your learning. When times are challenging, and the demands are high, quadruple your learning. Learning is a marvelous offense in a radically changing world.

Ironically, a history of professional success can decelerate growth. Satisfaction with the past and present inhibits accelerated learning and adaptability. Without shifting your attitudes to an insatiable quest for creative and expansive learning, you will lose your vitality by resting on the past. A continuum of learning insures the removal of complacency and an increase in competency. No matter how successful you are, without investing in your personal growth, the risk of sinking into repetitive and hypnotic activity is inevitable. The key to sustained success is to keep learning. Probe, adjust, adapt, and develop in new directions.

Look for people who will challenge you. No matter how competent you are, never allow your ego to swell to the point that you shut out the expertise of others. Enlist the help of a friend, a mentor to tell you truthfully where you can grow, expand your talents, or seek new possibilities. You want someone who will challenge you and inspire you to tackle the unknown. Such a friend will prove professionally invaluable.

Learn from your actions. Harvard Business School's John Kotter suggests, "You grab a challenge, act on it, then honestly reflect on why your actions worked or didn't. You learn from it and then move on. That continuous process of lifelong learning helps enormously in a rapidly changing economic environment."

I read about two guys who should have heeded the advice to learn from their actions. Jake and Joe were avid hunters. A week of hunting in the backwoods of Canada netted them each a large moose. When their pilot returned to retrieve them from the wilderness, he had an immediate concern. "I can't fly you out of here with all the gear and those two moose."

"Why not?" asked a surprised Joe.

"Because my plane doesn't have enough horsepower to carry such a load."

"But the plane that flew us out of here last year was exactly like this one," Jake protested.

"Really?" the pilot responded. "Well, I guess if you did it last year, I can do it, too."

They loaded the plane and began their takeoff. The plane crept across the water but struggled to climb out of the forest with all the weight and crashed into the mountain side.

Shaken but uninjured, the men crawled from the wreckage and Joe asked, "Where are we?"

Jake surveyed the surroundings and replied, "I'm not sure, but I guess we are about a mile farther than last year."

Learn from your experiences. If things don't work, don't keep doing them the same way, and expect positive results.

Today's organization has no pity on the person who is lackadaisical about learning. People are expected to take responsibility for updating their skills or be left in the dust. Becoming obsolete happens quickly without constant retooling. Your supervisor may be a great advocate for personal growth, but you will ultimately need to jump-start the internal drive to stay abreast of what's needed for you to acquire the necessary specialized knowledge. The more you know, the more valuable you become.

Eric Hofer believed, "In time of drastic change, it is the learners who inherit the future. The learned usually find themselves equipped to live in a world that no longer exists." Prepare now to be ready for your inheritance . . . the future.

GROW BEYOND WHERE
YOU ARE

*Only those who
constantly
retool
themselves
stand a chance
of staying
employed in the
years ahead.*

TOM PETERS

❋

Update your résumé. List all of your skills, talents, and unique abilities. Include both your personal and professional qualities. Don't break your arm patting yourself on the back, but do take time to review the achievements you've experienced.

Now, based on what you've written, ask yourself the following question: What have I done in the past 30 days to increase my competence in these areas and expand my capabilities?

The fulfilled professional and the one considered the most valuable by employers is an ever-growing, always expanding individual. Think beyond the basics you have mastered to new opportunities and challenges. Instead of locking your radar into a comfort zone, pursue the unknown. Gain insight into areas others have overlooked. Become inquisitive by exploring options for innovative changes and improvements.

Resting on past achievements is no longer acceptable and far from guaranteeing a promising career. Constant upgrading of skills is required to face the changing nature of the world around us. Job security isn't earned by showing up. We need to reformat our thinking around the value we offer to the organization. Feeling entitled to climbing another rung on the ladder, salary increases, or even maintaining our present positions is a defeating trap.

Become an expert at what you do. Constant retooling—perpetual learning—professional renewal—These are the tools of a marketable and competent professional. A relentless drive to effect work habits, improve your credentials, delve deeper into your interests, and maintain a thirst for never finishing your education.

My daughter is a dancer. I marvel at the effort it takes for her to achieve new levels of dance precision. Practice involves stretching muscles, coordinating graceful steps and distinct arm movements, pushing her limits, and all the while producing a smile that camouflages her discomfort.

The year-end dance recital creates excitement and anticipation for the performers to display the fruits of their efforts. Grueling hours of instruction and learning culminate into a parent-pleasing production. But none of this is possible without incremental, consistent growth.

Your recital is a daily performance that requires you to dream, dare, stretch, and risk outside the ordinary habitual ambitions. Don't let the past or present competencies evolve into future inadequacies. Work through the discomfort that often accompanies stretching. Remind yourself daily that the more you challenge yourself to expand beyond the customary comfort box, the easier your task will be when called upon to perform a crowd-pleasing production.

A friend asked Henry Wadsworth Longfellow the secret of his continued interest in life. Pointing to a nearby apple tree, he responded, "The purpose of that apple tree is to grow a little new wood each year. That is what I plan to do." I can handle professional growth when understood from Longfellow's perspective. Growing a little new wood each year protects us from stagnation and might even prompt us to grow a whole new branch.

Excelling requires us to move beyond past limitations and the present *status quo.* Reinvest your energies in the undiscovered, uncharted, unusual way of doing things.

Abandon the familiar ruts and overcome your addiction to ineffective ways of doing things. Create a new performance paradigm that yields a shift in the way you've always approached your job.

The more you know, the more you know how to do, the better you do it, the more valuable you become, and the more career satisfaction you'll attain.

*As long as you're green, you're growing; as soon as you're ripe, you start to rot.*

RAY KROC

❁

PREPARE FOR
THE FUTURE

The story is told of a man who realized he was slowly losing his memory. He sought the counsel of a doctor and, after a careful examination, the doctor said that an operation on his brain might reverse his condition and restore his memory. "However," the doctor said, "you must understand how delicate this surgery is. If one nerve is severed, total blindness could result."

A deafening silence filled the room.

"What would you rather have," asked the surgeon, attempting to break the uncomfortable silence, "your sight or your memory?"

The man pondered his choices for a few moments and then replied, "My sight, because I would rather see where I am going than remember where I have been."

This same mindset is endorsed by the person who understands how fast life is moving and, in order to survive and thrive, must move beyond the past. You can't forget your past but neither do you have to live in it. Jack Hayford, pastor of Church of the Way in Van Nuys, California commented, "The past is a dead issue, and we can't gain any momentum moving toward tomorrow if we are dragging the past behind us." As important as your past is, it is not so important as the way you see and prepare for the future. Therefore, our efforts should be directed toward refining our vision, not saving our memory.

Here are helpful hints for building your future:

**Know what you stand for.** I've encountered a lot of people in recent years who are troubled about tomorrow. People worry about what's coming next. What will they have to face? How can they measure up to increasing demands? How can they keep their lives on track?

Carrying around such heavy concerns can become a real burden. One anecdote for these anxieties is to know exactly for what you stand. What values and principles guide your life? Where are you willing to be flexible? In what areas is there no room for negotiation? Be clear about the boundaries that will provide a clear path for you to live your life.

**Double-check your perspective.** Where there is no hope in the future, we remain obsessed with the past. Where there is faith in the future, there is power to live today.

Fear is certainly a normal emotion when we look ahead. That's one reason why a lot of people keep living in the past. What's there to fear, I've already endured it all. There are a lot of uncontrollable variables when you begin anticipating tomorrow. But it is tomorrow where we will spend the rest of our lives and it is unhealthy and unnecessary to let fear remain in control.

There is a definite fascination with pointing out the inevitable downside of the future. I never cease to be amazed at the number of people who can catastrophize the smallest bad news into this generation's major depression. Dr. Norman Cousins advised, "One of the most important things in life is the need *not* to accept downside predictions from experts. It's true in interpersonal relationships just as it is true in business. No one knows enough to make a pronouncement of doom."

It's antiproductive to complain about possible future events. Substantial energy is lost resisting, being angry, or avoiding a future that challenges present assumptions and expectations. Maintain the faith, see the bigger picture, and invest your energies to seize potential opportunities.

**Be flexible.** Somebody once said, "Blessed are the flexible, for they shall not be bent out of shape." Here's a bit of advice that should go without saying, but it bears repeating: Be prepared that not everything in life will go according to your plan.

Considerable disappointment could be averted if people would look for new approaches when things don't go their way. Rather than bemoaning the unfairness of life, invest your energy in finding and seizing previously nonexistent, priceless opportunities. By catching on to this principle, you'll be better able to remain caught up with the pace of change.

Allow the virtues of hard work and positive anticipation to create a renewed sense of hope for future success.

**Focus on a vision for the future.** Fasten your seat belt. This step is going to take a fast track to some serious thought control and adjustment. Instead of worrying about or bemoaning all that could happen, get busy creating a vision of the future you want.

Peter Block, writing in *The Empowered Manager,* reminds us that, "We claim ownership over our lives when we identify the future that we want for ourselves and our unit. Our deepest commitment is to choose to live, to choose the destiny that has been handed to us, and to choose to pursue that destiny. These choices are expressed at work when we create a vision for our unit and decide to pursue that vision at all costs."

You will be far happier if you put the future to work for you rather than allowing the future to work you. Make next week, next year, and the coming decade your ally by determining what you want and setting your sights on achieving it. Keep the vision continually in front of you, review it frequently in your imagination, and determine specific actions that will move you closer each day.

In an essay entitled "Good Guys Finish First (Sometimes)," Andrew Bagnato told the following story:

Following a rags-to-riches season that led them to the Rose Bowl—their first in decades—Northwestern University's Wildcats met with coach Gary Barnett for the opening of spring training.

As players found their seats, Barnett announced that he was going to hand out the awards that many Wildcats had earned in 1995. Some players exchanged glances. Barnett does not normally dwell on the past. But as the coach continued to call players forward and handed them placards proclaiming their achievements, they were cheered on by their teammates.

One of the other coaches gave Barnett a placard representing his 17 national coach-of-the-year awards. Then, as the applause subsided, Barnett walked to a trash can marked "1995." He took an admiring glance at his placard, then dumped it in the can.

In the silence that followed, one by one, the team's stars dumped their placards on top of Barnett's. Barnett had shouted a message without uttering a word: "What you did in 1995 was terrific, lads. But look at the calendar: It's 1996."

André Gide suggested, "One doesn't discover new lands without consenting to lose sight of the shore for a very long time." Put the shore of yesterday behind you and begin stretching for a new horizon.

*Today is the first day of the rest of your life. So, it's no use fussing about the past because you can't do anything about it. But you have today, and today is when everything that's going to happen from now on begins.*

HARVEY FIRESTONE, JR.

## SETTLE FOR NOTHING LESS THAN WOW!

*Do what you do so well that those who see you do what you do are going to come back to see you do it again and tell others that they should see what you do.*

WALT DISNEY

❋

To achieve a level of "Wow" performance requires you to be more than average. You must go beyond what anyone would expect. Henry Ward Beecher believed that to achieve success, "Hold yourself responsible for a higher standard than anybody else expects of you."

"No one ever attains very eminent success by simply doing what is required of him," added Charles Kendall Adams. "It is the amount and excellence of what is over and above the required that determines greatness." Let me illustrate.

As a young father, Walt Disney would accompany his daughters on afternoon getaways to a local amusement park. While sitting on a dirty park bench, indulging in stale popcorn, rubbery hot dogs, and watered-down drinks, he dreamed of creating the ideal amusement park. He dreamed of a place where families around the world would be attracted to visit. From Mainstreet USA, to Pirates of the Caribbean, Disney thought through every intricate detail.

Quality food, cleanliness, attractive and inviting rides, and a variety of wholesome entertainment would be fun for everyone. This would be a family adventure second to none.

It took Walt 15 years to make his dream a reality. Even those closest to Disney found it hard to relate to his expansive vision. His own brother, Roy, thought the entire concept was a screwball idea. Walt encountered numerous obstacles and problems. It would have been easy to settle for something less than the ideal. But by the time Disneyland opened in 1955, the real thing was just as impressive as he had pictured it.

Thirty thousand people visited Disneyland on opening day. By the end of seven weeks, one million people had enjoyed Disney's creation. Today millions of people each year experience the fulfillment of Disney's own admonition: "Do what you do so well that those who see you do what you do are going to come back to see you do it again and tell others that they should see what you do."

Disney knew that if he didn't create a "Wow" experience, people would forget Disneyland existed and it would soon be considered just another run-of-the-mill amusement park. To avoid such a demise, the brass on

Disneyland's carousel is polished daily, the park benches always appear new due to frequent applications of paint, and the shooting gallery targets get a paint touch-up every night. The cleaning crew is extensively trained before assuming their incredible challenge and even the car parking crew is thoroughly instructed on Disney's commitment to courtesy.

No doubt about it, Walt Disney raised the bar on amusement park expectations. He began with a lofty vision of what could be, and persevered in selling that vision and the tangible result. Disney paid very close attention to details and challenged developers to continually find ways to improve on the design. His own personal high standards and self-discipline made it possible for those carrying on after him to create a "Wow" experience.

Willa A. Foster once said, "Quality is never an accident; it is always the result of high intention, sincere effort, intelligent direction, and skillful execution; it represents the wise choice of many alternatives." Simply stated: You will only be as good as the choices you make. Talent, circumstances, luck, heredity, environment, and personality are immaterial. What matters is how good you plan to be using what you have.

Personal and professional excellence requires 100 percent all the time. A passionate commitment 89, 93, or even 98 percent of the time reduces the "Wow" factor to acceptable or mediocre. Adequacy is an unstimulating goal to attain. If you want others to notice your efforts, make plans to do it better than you or they ever thought possible.

*My philosophy is that not only are you responsible for your life, but doing the best at this moment puts you in the best place for the next moment.*

OPRAH WINFREY

"No matter what you do, do it to your utmost," advised Russell H. Conwell. "I always attribute my success . . . to always requiring myself to do my level best, if only in driving a tack in straight." Enough said.

Successful people never settle for mediocrity or not using their abilities to the fullest. Zig Ziglar said, "Success is the maximum utilization of the ability that you have." Legendary basketball coach John Wooden concurs. "Success," he said, "comes from knowing that you did your best to become the best that you are capable of becoming." In that pursuit, it is impossible to be satisfied with anything less than excellence.

Since the day our children were old enough to understand, we instituted a cardinal rule in our home. It wasn't always a popular rule because it held the children accountable for their actions. The rule? Approach every ball game, school challenge, dance competition, musical performance, or any other day-to-day life experience with a sincere commitment to give your best. My wife and I never required our children to be the best, the smartest, or the fastest. However, they would tell you there was an inexcusable expectation that they would give, perform, and be the best they could be.

Remember Nadia Comaneci? She was the first gymnast ever to earn a perfect score in Olympic competition. I remember watching that flawless performance during the 1976 Olympics in Montreal. It was impossible not to get excited about her performance and the gold medal.

In a later interview, Comaneci explained the expectations she set for herself and how she was able to maintain such a high standard of performance: "I always underestimated what I did by saying, 'I can do better.' To be an Olympic champion you have to be a little abnormal and work harder than everyone else. Being normal is not great because you will have a boring life. I live by a code I created: Don't pray for an easy life. Pray to be a strong person."

Successful people go beyond what others consider acceptable. They do more than others expect, set standards that stretch them beyond their last performance, pay attention to the smallest details, and are willing to go the extra mile that pushes them outside the box of mediocrity. Being your best never happens by accident. You have to make it happen and that begins with an attitude that accepts personal responsibility for the methods and results you experience.

*Sometimes I worry about being a success in a mediocre world.*

LILY TOMLIN

❋

# BECOME THE "OWN" IN OWNERSHIP

*The secret to success on the job is to work as though you were working for yourself. Your company provides you with the work area, equipment and other benefits, but basically you know what has to get done and the best way to do it, so it's up to you to run your own show.*

LAIR RIBEIRO

*Success Is No Accident*

ACT LIKE
AN OWNER

Calculate the hours you spend at work, and you'll quickly realize your job represents a major part of your life. It requires a huge investment, so working for just a paycheck and a few benefits will provide only temporary work enjoyment. In fact, one of the worst mistakes you can make is to think you are working for someone else.

Andy Grove, Intel Corporation's CEO, gave a group of graduates from the University of California at Berkeley some sound advice. He said, "Accept that no matter where you go to work, you are not an employee—you are a business with one employee, you. Nobody owes you a career. You own it, as a sole proprietor. You must compete with millions of individuals every day of your career. You must enhance your value every day, hone your competitive advantage, learn, adapt, move jobs and industries—retrench so you can advance, learn new skills. So you do not become one of those

*Always accept yourself as self-employed and look upon every single thing you accomplish or don't accomplish as your own responsibility.*
BRIAN TRACY

statistics in 2015. And remember: This process starts on Monday."

Here's how you can activate an ownership lifestyle. Assume the presidency of your own personal corporation. Accept responsibility for the results you generate and continually seek resolutions to performance problems and productivity barriers. A natural outcome will be that your performance advances to the next level. You are ultimately accountable for the quality of your work and the fulfillment you experience. Challenge yourself to do whatever it takes to be successful and take responsibility for failures. No matter who signs your paycheck, in the final analysis, you work for yourself.

**Invest yourself passionately in what you do.** There is no room in today's marketplace for people who punch in, half-heartedly go through eight hours of repetitive motions, and punch out. Take charge of your morale. Don't depend on the organization or someone else to pump you up. No one possesses the power to keep you inspired. Fill your own energy tank. Immersed in what you do as an owner, you create a unique capacity to enjoy the adventure of work for extended periods of time.

**Never confuse longevity with contribution.**
Tenure is important if you continue to add value to your department and/or the organization. I feel sorry for people who live under the mistaken assumption that longevity qualifies them for security, additional salary, or added privileges. It just doesn't work that way. Organizations simply don't take the personal interest in people's careers like they did in the past. Most of us are primarily on our own.

Loyalty to your company is valuable but you don't get extra credit for "putting in your time." Look outside your job description to find ways to contribute more to the organization than you cost. Do more than you are asked. Stay later than is expected of you. Search for ways to increase your worth to the organization far beyond what you are being paid. Make it evident that you would be missed if you weren't there. If you can't identify specific things you have done to profit your company in this way, get your résumé updated.

**Think in terms of partnership.** J.C. Penney once declared, "I will have no man work for me who has not the capacity to become a partner." Inspire other people to make things happen. Look for ways to cultivate cooperative relationships. Assume more personal responsibility for the success of the entire organization. Create a vision of what your department could become. How can you personally cut costs, improve productivity, eliminate waste, serve the customer better, and improve the emotional well-being of the company?

**Embrace the demands of change.** Organizations need high-performance people. It is virtually impossible to stay on the cutting-edge of your profession without continual, and, oftentimes, rapid growth. Become a master at what you do and then do whatever it takes to stay abreast of what is happening in your field. The choice is to either be a perpetual student who continually acquires new skills or become outdated and obsolete.

Learn to deal with ambiguity and uncertainty. Pro-actively endorse shifting and expanding responsibilities. Remain fluid and flexible. Improvise as necessary and accept the fact that times are changing and things are not returning to "normal." Feel your way down the path to the future and remain answerable for your actions. Become self-empowered. Discover your untapped potential.

Behaving like you're in business for yourself frees you to capitalize on possibilities and be accountable for outcomes.

This is a marvelous opportunity to shine in your position, develop an entrepreneurial reputation, and make a significant difference for those who pay for your work.

## TAKE THE TIME TO
## FIX YOUR LEAKY BOAT

*The rule of accuracy: When working toward the solution of a problem it always helps if you know the answer.*

JOHN PEER

❁

Here's some news you'll love to hear: Problems are a part of every job. Of course, that's nothing new to you. What's important is whether you decide to do something about your problems or just be satisfied to complain about them. It's easy to get so caught up in your trials and tribulations that you fail to get beyond them.

I love the story of a man in a rowboat about 25 yards offshore. He's rowing like crazy but getting nowhere. A woman standing on the nearby shore sees the man is in trouble and notices the rowboat has a bad leak and is slowly sinking. She shouts to the man, but he's too busy bailing water to answer her. She shouts louder; he continues to row and bail. Finally she yells at the top of her lungs, "Hey, if you don't get the boat ashore and fix the leak, you're going to drown!"

"Thanks, lady," the man replies, "but I don't have time to fix the leak."

We all encounter situations when it takes every ounce of energy we have just to stay afloat. Bailing and rowing become the dominant activities. If we would only take the time to fix the source of our problem, rather than just desperately attack the symptoms, we might not be so worn out at the end of the day. Every job requires us to go ashore periodically to fix our leaky boats.

Problems are as natural as the sun coming up in the morning and going down at night. You'll see plenty of them in your career. Build a reputation as a problem-solver, and you'll be considered a valuable person on the team. Here are a few strategies to consider as you become a leak fixer.

**Admit there is a leak.** "Stubbornness in refusing to recognize a problem has destroyed a lot of bottom lines," observed Harvey Mackay. "You can't solve a problem unless you first admit you have one."

In his book *Identity: Youth and Crisis,* Erik Erikson tells a story he got from a physician about a man with a peculiar situation. The old man vomited every morning but had never felt any inclination to consult a doctor. Finally, the man's family convinced him to get checked out.

The doctor asked, "How are you?"

"I'm fine," the man responded. "Couldn't be better."

The doctor examined him and found he was in good shape for his age. Finally, the physician grew impatient and asked, "I hear that you vomit every morning."

The old man looked surprised and said, "Sure. Doesn't everybody?"

Some people don't realize the problems they live with are abnormal. They have been dealing with them for so long, they've convinced themselves that everyone has a leaky boat.

"Recognizing a problem doesn't always bring a solution," James Baldwin reminds us, "but until we recognize that problem, there can be no solution."

**Be realistic about the size of the hole.** Many times people look at a problem telescopically so the leak looks bigger than it actually is. As E.W. Howe wrote in *Success Is Easier Than Failure,* "Some people storm imaginary Alps all their lives, and die in the foothills cursing difficulties that do not exist." Out of such instances arose the popular "don't make a mountain out of a molehill" advice. American publisher Al Neuharth said, "The difference between a mountain and a molehill is your perspective."

A businessperson experienced a drastic downturn in sales, and the possibility of shutting down was a real threat. When a friend asked how he was doing, the man replied, "Times are so tough I'm getting several calls a day from national leaders."

The friend was taken back a bit and asked, "Why are they calling you?"

The down-in-the-mouth executive replied, "They enjoy talking with someone who has bigger problems than they do."

John Maxwell believes, "People need to change their perspectives, not their problems." Don't exaggerate the enormity of your problems. Overreacting or "catastrophizing" puts the power in the problem rather than your ability to solve it. Be suspicious of the power and control you've given any challenge.

**Don't wait for a lifeguard.** Accept responsibility for the problems you are experiencing and you can begin to rise above the crisis. Wait for a lifeguard to rescue you, and you may drown before help arrives.

A critical mistake many people make is assigning fault for a problem and then removing themselves from any responsibility for resolving it. If you're in the boat and the boat springs a leak, whose problem is it? Even though the leak might have been created by someone else, it would be wise for you to make some adjustments or be willing to accept the annoyances, conflict, or drowning the leak will cause.

A problem is something you can do something about. If you fail to do something about it, it will become a fact of life and then you will need to learn to live with it. Because we've gotten so good at the blame game and avoiding personal responsibility, we've become victims by our own choices.

Comedian and actor W.C. Fields once said, "Remember, a dead fish can float downstream, but it takes a live one to swim upstream." It takes minimal effort or skill to point an accusing finger at other people. What difference does it make now to blame others? The problem is yours and is in need of corrective action.

The truly effective person is the one who can navigate upstream, against the flow of irresponsibility and finger-pointing, toward workable solutions. It's your boat you're sitting in. Take ownership for its condition. Don't focus on the leak. That only produces fear, anger, desperation, or paralysis. Trapped in those emotional reactions, the clarity of the ideal solution is blurred. Tap into your experience and insight to discover how best to solve the leak.

**Find a plug that fills the hole.** I love the story of the old country doctor who was giving a patient an examination. At the conclusion, he scratched his head and asked in bewilderment, "Have you had this before?"

"Yes, I have," the patient replied.

The doctor looked his patient in the eye and said, "Well, you've got it again."

The epitome of frustration comes from the continual analysis of a problem without a proper diagnosis and plan of action. You can stare at a hole in the boat and repeat to yourself over and over, "Yep, there's a hole in the boat," but until a course of correction is set, this risk of sinking remains.

John Foster Dulles, Secretary of State during the Eisenhower administration, suggested that, "The measure of success is not whether you have a tough problem to deal with, but whether it's the same problem you had last year." Thomas J. Watson, Jr., former head of IBM, said, "I never varied from the managerial rule that the worst possible thing we could do would be to lie dead in the water with any problem. Solve it, solve it quickly, solve it right or wrong. If you solved it wrong, it would come back and slap you in the face and then you could solve it right. Doing nothing is a comfortable alternative because it is without immediate risk, but it is an absolutely fatal way to manage a business."

Pastor and author A.B. Simpson told the story of a farmer who plowed around a large rock in his field year after year. He had broken several pieces of equipment by running into it. Each time he saw that rock sprawled out in his field, he grumbled about how much trouble it had caused.

One day the farmer decided to dig up the rock and do away with it for good. Putting a large crowbar under one side, he began prying and soon discovered, much to his surprise, that the rock was less than a foot thick. Within a short period of time, he had removed the rock from the field and hauled it away in his wagon. He smiled to think how that "monstrous" rock had caused him so much frustration.

Quit plowing around your problems. They will still be there tomorrow. We don't need the same old problems reoccurring day after day after day. New challenges are continually coming your way and the cumulative affect of new and old problems can be overwhelming. Sigmund Freud stated, "A man with a toothache cannot be in love." Why? Because he spends all his time thinking about the toothache.

Dispose of the old hassles. Work through them. Search for alternative approaches. Make some decisions. Find solutions. Take care of them so you can move on to new opportunities.

**Understand the value of leaks.** Problems are a natural, inevitable condition for growth. All growth produces problems but not all problems produce growth. The difference is your understanding of that truth. Lloyd Ogilvie, writing in his book *If God Cares, Why Do I Still Have Problems,* suggests, "The greatest problem we all share, to a greater or lesser degree, is a profound misunderstanding of the positive purpose of problems. Until we grapple with this gigantic problem, we will be helpless victims of our problems all through our life."

Problems are a source of instruction, insight, and opportunity. When we learn to look at them correctly, the challenge of meeting those problems head on keeps us alive, vibrant, and on our toes. Problems stimulate the development of our mind and talents while stretching us to new levels of thinking and performance. Reacting foolishly, resenting problems, or avoiding them will keep you from experiencing the benefits they can bring.

*The best way to eat the elephant standing in your path is to cut it up into little pieces.*

AFRICAN
PROVERB

❋

In *The Road Less Traveled,* best-selling author Scott Peck offers this valuable perspective on problems: "It is in this whole process of meeting and solving problems that life has meaning. Problems are the cutting edge that distinguishes between success and failure. Problems call forth our courage and our wisdom; indeed they create our courage and our wisdom. It is only because of problems that we grow mentally and spiritually. It is through the pain of confronting and resolving problems that we learn. As Benjamin Franklin said, 'Those things that hurt, instruct.'"

Look with an open mind for the value in each challenge you encounter. Every miracle in the Bible began with a problem. So, when you find yourself surrounded by water in your leaking boat, implement the suggestions you've just read and keep in mind that you are a candidate for a miracle.

## DON'T HOLD
## BACK

I realize that no matter what anyone says, some people will always embrace Mark Twain's attitude when he said, "I do not like work even when someone else does it." However, I'm also convinced that most of us are interested in erasing any possibility for a vague and undefined work life. The simple fact is, we want more than a paycheck.

I predict there are very few people in the world who get up in the morning, shower, dress, have a little breakfast, and announce, "I can't wait to do a really *bad* job today."

Yet, surveys indicate nearly 85 percent of the workers in the United States say they could work harder on the job, and nearly half claim they could double their effectiveness.

Too many people are not emotionally committed to the importance of what they do. The job is often blamed but that is absurd. For every person complaining about his or her job, there are several others investing themselves in those perceived mundane experiences.

*There's a difference between interest and commitment. When you're interested in doing something, you do it only when it is convenient. When you are committed to something, you accept no excuses, only results.*

KEN
BLANCHARD
❀

Every organization has people who always do less than they are told; still others who will do what they are told, but no more; and some who will do things without being told. What organizations need more of is the minority group who actually inspire others to do things. These are people who constantly renew their own commitment to being their best.

The world has little room for people who put in their time, go through the motions with a half-hearted effort, and are careless, sloppy, or even indifferent. A grand prize for showing up and going through the motions is not in the cards. The uncommitted are left in the dust.

In today's world, people who eliminate excuses, pro-actively work from the heart, invest themselves passionately in what they do, and apply their skills and talents to the fullest are maximizing their professional potential.

President Eisenhower, while addressing the National Press Club, opened his remarks by apologizing that he was not a great orator. He likened his situation to a boyhood experience on a Kansas farm.

Eisenhower recalled, "An old farmer had a cow that we wanted to buy. We went over to visit him and asked about the cow's pedigree. The old farmer didn't know what pedigree meant, so we asked him about the cow's butterfat production. He told us that he hadn't any idea. Finally, we asked him if he knew how many pounds of milk the cow produced each year. The farmer shook his head and said, 'I don't know. But she's an honest old cow and she'll give you all the milk she has!'"

Eisenhower then concluded his opening remarks, "Well, I'm like the cow: I'll give you everything I have."

That is a pure and simple commitment. When the urge to slough off arises or you're on the verge of giving less than your best, consider Eisenhower's pledge. Giving everything you have makes work far more satisfying. It's a great anecdote for boredom as well as stress and is ultimately a gift you give to yourself.

*Commitment unlocks the doors of imagination, allows vision and gives us the 'right stuff' to turn our dreams into reality.*

JAMES WOMACK

❀

# GIVE YOUR BEST
## TO WHAT
## MATTERS MOST

*Time only runs in one direction and seems
to do so in an orderly fashion.*

PATRICIA CORNWELL

**B**ernard Benson once commented, "I wish I could stand on a busy corner, hat in hand, and beg people to throw me all their wasted hours." There's a good chance he'd become a wealthy man given the opportunity to fulfill his wish. I doubt there is anything people waste more of than time.

Time-management expert Michael Fortino launched an in-depth study called the Fortino Efficiency Index. Fortino discovered that during the course of a lifetime, the average American spends . . .

- One year looking for misplaced objects
- Eight months opening junk mail
- Two years trying to return phone calls of people who never seem to be in
- Five years standing in line (at the bank, movie theater, etc.)

Additional research by Tor Dahl, chairperson of the World Confederation of Productivity Science, indicates that the average American business wastes or misdirects work time as follows:

- 23 percent waiting for approvals, materials, or support
- 20 percent doing things that shouldn't even be done
- 15 percent doing things that should be handled by someone else
- 18 percent doing things wrong
- 16 percent for failing to do the right things

Do any of those sound familiar? You can probably list additional daily activities that rob you of valuable time. Just being aware of and sensitive to avoiding wasted minutes and hours can provide a fresh perspective of time.

My intent is not to offer a cure-all for the epidemic of lost time. I am interested in offering you an assorted selection of antibiotics you can draw on to treat this infection. Although our lack of effectiveness and efficiency can be hindered by a number of external infecting agents, we are ultimately responsible for dealing with the causes and symptoms. Time is your personal possession. Nobody can manage it or fix it for you. You are in control. You can do something. Your life is yours and you can choose to live it with greater control and healthy time usage.

You might be plagued with a lack of self discipline, indecisiveness, or even personal disorganization. Maybe the cause of time slipping by is daydreaming, poor delegation skills, an inability to say no, or a lack of priorities. Whatever the case, here is a plethora of ideas for you to consider. Give immediate attention to those that cause an "Aha" reaction.

**1. Ask the right question.** First and foremost, when involved in any activity that hints of wasted time, ask yourself, "Is this the best way for me to be spending my time right now?" Then, act accordingly.

**2. Schedule work according to your peak productivity time.** Designate those hours you are most productive to doing things that give the highest return and produce the greatest value. The German poet Goethe put it this way: "The key to life is concentration and elimination."

**3. Determine your priorities.** You can't do everything. Overambitious to-do lists can be unrealistic and antiproductive. Make choices. Sort out your "have-to's" from your "choose-to's." You'll be amazed how many times you choose to do rather than have to do. Direct your energies toward activities that are the most important to you.

Robert Eliot suggested, "It's important to run not on the fast track, but on your track. Pretend you only have six months to live, and make three lists: the things you *have* to do, *want* to do, and neither have to do nor want to do. Then, for the rest of your life, forget everything on the third list."

**4. Be result oriented rather than activity oriented.** Activity does not equal accomplishment. "No other principle of effectiveness is violated as constantly today as the basic principle of concentration," said Peter Drucker. "Our motto seems to be, 'let's do a little bit of everything.'" Measure your effectiveness by what you achieve, not by how busy you are.

**5. Get organized.** According to Albert R. Karr, writing in the *Wall Street Journal,* "Executives waste nearly six weeks a year looking for misplaced items, according to a poll of 200 large-company executives for Accountemps, a temporary help firm." Have a place for everything, and have everything in its place.

**6. Get up earlier.** By rising 30 minutes earlier each day, you add 3-$\frac{1}{2}$ hours of productivity to your week. Multiply that by 52 weeks and you'll have an additional 180 hours to accomplish your priorities. I've used these extra hours to write books, design seminars, and get energized spiritually by reading inspirational material or spending time in prayer.

**7. Learn to say no.** Busy people must simply learn to refuse some demands made on their time. It's natural not to want to disappoint people. Sometimes we're unrealistic about our limits. It's easy to let our ego get in the way of saying no; the need to be needed is a powerful decision influence. You'll never feel in control if you're biting off more than you can chew.

**8. Work on your attitude.** Your attitude about how busy you are, the amount of time you have, or the demands on your life can sabotage any effort to make the most of the time you have. Be flexible. Not everything will go as expected. Seek new opportunities when your game plan runs into road blocks.

**9. Quit daydreaming.** Turn mind wandering into action.

**10. Do things right the first time.** If you don't have time to do it right, when will you have time to do it over?

**11. Plan ahead.** For instance, lay your clothes out for the next day before you go to bed at night, purchase holiday or birthday presents in advance, and keep tabs on special days and events 30 days in advance.

**12. Place deadlines on yourself.** Don't allow minor or major projects to drag on indefinitely. Challenge yourself with deadlines, and beat them.

**13. Prepare for unexpected down time.** Spare minutes created by waiting in airports, restaurants, traffic, etc., can be the perfect time to indulge in small projects.

**14. Manage meetings.** Use a specific time like 9:13 or 1:32 to start your meetings and set a predetermined time for adjournment. Stay on task.

**15. Don't put off until the day after tomorrow what you can do today.** Procrastination is an ugly, frustrating habit. Do it today.

The philosopher and poet Goethe said, "We have time enough if we will but use it aright." Time is a precious commodity. It is available to all of us in equal parts to use as we choose. Time is like a talent—you can't produce more of it but you can make the most of what you have. To get the most out of each day, learn to savor each moment and make the most of every hour. Now would be a good time to take a minute to evaluate how you spend your hours.

*Don't put off for tomorrow what you can do today, because if you enjoy it today, you can do it again tomorrow.*

JAMES A. MICHENER

## LEARN TO SCHEDULE
## YOUR PRIORITIES

*The reason most major goals are not achieved is that we spend our time doing second things first.*

ROBERT MCKAIN

❋

Notice the title doesn't read "prioritize your schedule." Instead, decide what you want to spend your time doing. What are the most important elements of your life and work? Establish your priorities and then stick to them. Schedule them into your routine.

Unless you live congruently with your priorities, you will never feel in balance. You'll always have that nagging feeling that you're in a rat race you can't win. Awareness of and commitment to our priorities increases performance and productivity. With increasing forces pulling us in every direction, this principle is more important than ever.

Allow sufficient time and energy to enjoy the experiences, people, and activities you value most. This is the simplest yet most profound foundation for a successful life. All other goals and strategies for attaining them will fall into place when you live by the values you profess.

Don't be tempted or driven by distractions. Jumping from one thing to the next is the result of an undisciplined commitment to priorities. You don't have the emotional resources or physical energy to sufficiently support every worthy ideal vying for your attention.

Each day we are given the gift of 24 hours—1,440 minutes—86,400 seconds. Only one person can decide how this gift will be used. However we decide to invest our time communicates to others the values we espouse. You may argue that is not true of you. I would challenge you to consider this question: "Am I satisfied with the amount and quality of time I am giving to the important priorities in my life?" Don't immediately answer that, but ponder it for a few days.

Whenever we decide to do one thing, we have made a decision not to give our attention to something else. Time management, or life management for that matter, is a series of choices.

My fascination with the circus led me to discover the secret of the lion tamer's success. I found that, along with the whip and pistol strapped to his belt, the lion tamer's key tool is a four-legged stool. The stool is held by the back and the legs are thrust toward the face of the lion. Apparently the wild animal attempts to focus on all four legs at once, thereby overwhelming its senses. The lion is left paralyzed, tamed, and unable to aggressively respond. Sound familiar? Focus. Focus. Focus.

What are the top five personal priorities in your life? What are your five most important professional responsibilities? Now evaluate how much time you have given to each in the past six months. Are the hours and days adding up to the quality of life you desire?

If sufficient time and energy have been allocated for these priorities, you probably sense a degree of balance. Life feels in sync. If, on the other hand, these priorities are pushed on the back burner, I would wager there is a feeling of incompleteness and dissatisfaction.

Please note the wording of this strategy. I'm not suggesting a prioritizing of all daily responsibilities, activities, and events. Rather, based on your purpose, determine your top personal and professional priorities. Now schedule them into your weekly calendar. Religiously make sure these priorities are given top billing.

Most people don't have trouble listing their priorities. Few people seem to be able to give sufficient time to them.

We have good intentions. We make a gallant effort for a few weeks, but then tend to fall back into the habit of allowing our calendars to dictate our priorities, and soon life is out of sync.

I was involved in a greenhouse operation that raised 2,800 tomato plants. For us to raise the highest quality tomatoes took considerable maintenance. Little shoots at the bottom of the plant had to be trimmed or they would drain nutrients from the main stem. By trimming the "suckers," the remainder of the plant receives proper nourishment, thereby producing luscious fruit.

Our automatic watering system insured each plant received sufficient moisture to keep it healthy. Without the water, the plants would shrivel up and die. We had the labor and nutritional resources to support each plant.

Snip off your time suckers. Let them go. Nourish the fruit-producing priorities. Give them your energetic attention and celebrate the results.

Donald Rumsfeld suggested: "Control your own time. Don't let it be done for you. If you are working on the in-box that is fed you, you are probably working on the priority of others." Put into action today a plan that will allow you to choose how the precious gift of time will be spent.

*Things that matter most must never be at the mercy of things that matter least.*

JOHANN WOLFGANG VON GOETHE

❋

—————

I KNOW YOU'RE BUSY,
BUT WHAT ARE YOU GETTING DONE?

—————

Our high school Spanish Club sold candy to raise money for a trip to Mexico. The sponsoring teacher reminded each student how important it was to contact as many people as possible about buying the candy. "We've got ten days to make this fund-raiser successful," the teacher instructed. "I want to know at the end of those ten days how many contacts you made. Good luck."

As the students brought in their orders, one girl was bragging about her success. "I called on 74 houses door to door in one night. I started right after school and didn't even stop for supper. I would have been able to do more but a couple of people stopped me and wanted to buy."

In our fast-paced world it is easy to get caught up in a fury of activity. Observe people around you. Some are rushing here and there, attending one meeting after another, attempting to concentrate on several activities or projects at one time, writing reports, talking on the phone, eating on the run, and accomplishing very little.

The world doesn't care, whether you like it or not, how busy you are. The world doesn't reward you for how smart you are, your good intentions, or the dreams you hope to pursue.

What's important are results, what you have actually done. Far too often, we pat ourselves on the back for running in place even though the finish line is as far away at the end of the day as when we started the day. People who get things done will reap more than a self-appreciating pat on the back.

Making the transformation from being one who dilly-dallies throughout the day to one who makes a contribution involves an evaluation of current activity. Henry Ford said, "The number of needless tasks that are performed daily by thousands of people is amazing." He had a list of them, including:

- They make too many phone calls.
- They visit too often and stay too long on each visit.
- They write letters that are three times as long as necessary.

- They work on little things, neglect big ones.

- They read things that neither inform or inspire them.

- They have too much fun, too often.

- They spend hours with people who cannot stimulate them.

- They read every word of advertising circulars.

- They pause to explain why they did what they did, when they should be working on the next thing.

- They hurry to the movies when they should be going to night school.

- They daydream at work when they should be planning ahead for their job.

- They spend time and energy on things that don't count.

Sound a bit harsh? No one can probably meet these standards all day every day. They are worthy guidelines, however, when we get caught in the activity trap. No one feels like being productive every day. But a bit more focus might result in substantial fulfillment.

Forget your excuses, lack of energy, aches and pains, and obsession with being busy. Do the things you know you have to do to achieve the results you want to achieve, and become the person you want to be.

*A fellow doesn't last long on what he has done. He's got to keep on delivering as he goes along.*

CARL
HUBBELL

# TAP INTO YOUR TALENT

*If a man has talent and cannot use it, he
has failed. If he has a talent and uses only
half of it, he has partly failed. If he has
a talent and learns somehow to use the
whole of it, he has gloriously succeeded
and won satisfaction and a triumph few
men and women ever know.*

THOMAS WOLFE

## FOCUS ON
## WHAT YOU DO BEST

A n agency rep was presented the challenge of coming up with a campaign to boost the sales of a popular laundry soap. The product had enjoyed strong customer approval for many years. What more could be said that hadn't already been discovered by users?

One day he poured a box of the soap on the top of his desk, hoping to discover something that would prompt his creativity. Suddenly, he noticed the soap was full of little blue crystals. He immediately went to the manufacturer to find out what the blue crystals were all about. What he learned sparked a successful campaign, significantly increasing sales. The blue crystals supplied the soap with super-whitening, brightening agents that made the soap so effective.

Maybe you remember the ad pitch: "Try Tide—With the New Blue Crystals." Even though the crystals had always been there, it wasn't until their purpose and effectiveness was exposed that Tide received recognition for its super-cleaning powers.

*Talent without discipline is like an octopus on roller skates. There's plenty of movement, but you never know if it's going to be forward, backwards, or sideways.*

H. JACKSON
BROWN

❋

I work with people every day who are like Tide. Contained inside of them is an important element whose unique value has not been exposed. They are good at what they do, but if they ever realize the latent abilities waiting to be discovered, significant achievements await them. There are gifts waiting to be opened and used.

Excellence is touched when gifts are discovered, activated, and continually repeated. How else can we explain the repeated achievements of basketball great Michael Jordan, country music star Garth Brooks, homerun king Mark McGwire, best-selling novelist Tom Clancy, actor Robin Williams, golfers Jack Nicklaus or Tiger Woods, talk-show host Oprah Winfrey, or a host of other less-renown successful people? Achievers have learned to identify, appreciate, and develop their talents by seeking opportunities to use them. Their efforts are concentrated on practicing, enjoying, and refining the gifts they have discovered.

What does this mean for common, everyday people like us? Everyone is created with the equal ability to become an unequal. Although we're not all created equal, each of us possesses the capacity to stand out from the crowd in some area of our life. One of the basic elements of success is to be good at what you do. You won't be good at what you do unless you polish your skills and perfect your moves. Master the talents you possess. Be determined to live as a "will be," not a "has been."

On Tuesday, April 18, 1995, sports fans around the country had to be a bit saddened to watch superstar Joe Montana retire from professional football after 16 seasons. Twenty thousand fans gathered in downtown San Francisco for the retirement ceremonies.

Sportscasters, coaches, and players offered their accolades to one of the league's greatest quarterbacks. However, it wasn't always like this. When Joe Montana was recruited as a third-round draft pick out of Notre Dame, San Francisco fans were less than impressed. Montana was labeled with a variety of unflattering labels.

In an answer to his critics, Joe Montana entered the league and quickly began throwing passes with perfect timing. He redefined the two-minute drill. To those who said he was too weak and scrawny to play in the big leagues, he endured season after season of physical abuse. Then, he simply went on to lead the 49'ers to four Super Bowls and helped them become a feared and dominant team in the 1980s.

*Identify what's holding you back from being great. Then go out and work on turning your weaknesses into strengths.*

TERRY BRADSHAW

❋

Joe Montana will never be considered a "has been" because of his deliberate commitment to be what he "could be." Montana initially impressed very few people, but his consistent commitment to focus on what he could do best landed him in the record books and earned him the respect of the fans.

Johann Wolfgang von Goethe once said, "The man who is born with a talent which he has meant to use finds his greatest happiness in using it." To experience ongoing happiness and success with your career, find that talent that brings you joy and fulfillment.

You might say that a peak performer is a person exploring the farther reaches of his or her abilities. Push yourself to develop your talent beyond any level you may have achieved in the past.

## ACHIEVEMENT HAS
## NO FINISH LINE

chievers possess a dedication to action that continually expands their potential and increases their value. "Our business in life," said Steward Johnson, "is not to get ahead of others, but to get ahead of ourselves—to break our own records, to outstrip our yesterday by our today." Such a lifestyle requires a commitment beyond what most people are willing to make.

John Wesley committed 64 years of his life to being an uncommon achiever for God. He had no interest in being better than other preachers—he just tended to the business of being his best.

Wesley preached 42,400 sermons, averaging 15 sermons per week for 54 years. He traveled 290,000 miles (equal to circling the globe 20 times) on foot or on horseback. No jet services were available to whisk him across the miles. Travel, combined with his speaking schedule, was a true test of endurance. He was a prolific author. Wesley's works,

_Peak performers do not see accomplishment as a fixed state. One of their most engaging characteristics is an infectious talent for moving into the future, generating new challenges, living with a sense of work to be done._
CHARLES
GARFIELD

including translations, amounted to over 200 volumes. When John Wesley died, at age 88, it is said he left a worn coat, a battered hat, a humble cottage, a tattered Bible, and the Methodist Church.

Wesley never considered himself as "having arrived." New sermons, spiritually hungry people, inspired vision, and the internal drive to serve captured his energy. Although the summary of your life might seem minuscule compared with John Wesley's, what you can do is achieve a little more today than you did yesterday. Work tomorrow to exceed yesterday's expectations.

Personal achievement has no finish line. As milestones are attained, encouraging you to continue, remain cautious of the temptation to put your life in neutral. Mediocrity, boredom, and uninspired standards will ultimately creep in and infect you. The antidote for these calamities is setting your sights on new peaks to scale, challenges to confront, or opportunities to master. Press on.

Set higher standards for achievement than anyone else around you. Compete with yourself to attain higher levels of performance. Unless you undertake more than you can possibly do, you will never do all you can do. This is a critical step to ongoing self-improvement that will jump-start your attitude and increase results. Self-directed pressure keeps you excited, energetic, and eager to attain heightened levels of performance.

Thomas Edison once said, "Three great essentials to achieve anything worthwhile are, first, hard work; second, stick-to-itiveness; third, common sense." I think I've adequately addressed hard work. It is summed up beautifully by James Allen: "He who would accomplish little must sacrifice little; he who would achieve much must sacrifice much."

What about stick-to-itiveness? George Bernard Shaw waited nine long years before he got anything published. Editors kept turning down everything he submitted. Undaunted by rejection, Shaw persistently kept working, writing, submitting, believing, and hoping. He also kept getting better at writing and, ultimately, got something published.

Zig Ziglar, commenting on Shaw's experience, had this observation: "Several factors are important. . . . Shaw believed that he had ability. He patiently persisted in honing his skills and pursuing publishers until finally somebody said yes. That's a good procedure to follow. If you really believe in what you're doing and have confidence that it is significant, you persist until something positive happens, knowing that it's always darkest just before the dawn."

It's easy to get fired up about a dream or goal for a short period of time. Sustaining passion in the face of adversity, rejection, or failure is the stuff of which achievers are made. Studies indicate that the one quality all successful people have is persistence. Joyce Brothers sees successful people as ". . . willing to spend more time accomplishing a task and to persevere in the face of many difficult odds. There's a very positive relationship between people's ability to accomplish any task and the time they're willing to spend on it." The power to press on in spite of everything, the power to endure—this is the achiever's quality. Persistency is the ability to face defeat, challenges, and disappointments again and again without giving up—to push on, knowing that you can attain your dreams, or at least a portion of them. Be willing to take the pains to overcome every obstacle, and to do whatever it takes.

The most vivid regrets in my life are those times when I quit too soon. A perceived lack of confidence, energy, or talent caused me to give up without realizing the fulfillment of a plan. I've since realized that any fulfillment worth its salt requires me to do the tough stuff first and realize satisfaction or reward down the road. Even when the odds are stacked against me, I've learned to overcome them by sustaining the best effort I know how.

Hang in there! Make stick-to-itiveness your ally.

I hesitate to bring up Edison's recommendation for common sense, as I don't think it can be taught. It is attained only through the practical lessons learned by everyday living. People who glean information from their life experiences and are capable of applying those lessons the next time they encounter similar situations, refine their sense of what works and what doesn't.

My advice is to thoughtfully progress along the road to your ultimate goals. Hastiness, reckless pursuit, ignoring yield and stop signs, and illogical turns rarely pay off. Stay the course. Make decisions based on the experiences you've endured.

Achievement may have no finish line, but achievers cross the line of short-term reward into a lifestyle of challenge and gratification. Every day recharges their spirit and catapults them into new ventures to enjoy.

## DIG A LITTLE
## DEEPER

The time was the Great Depression. The place was a sheep ranch in Texas. Owner, Mr. Yates, was having severe financial difficulties and on the brink of bankruptcy. Then an oil company, believing there might be oil on his land, asked for permission to drill.

Desperate, and feeling he had nothing to lose, Mr. Yates agreed to their request. A short time later, just below the surface, the oil drillers discovered the largest oil deposit found at that time on the North American continent. Overnight, Mr. Yate's financial difficulties disappeared. He was a billionaire.

The amazing thing about this account is that the untapped wealth was there all along. He just didn't realize it.

Now, let's take this illustration a bit further. Alfred Armand Montapert, writing in *The Superior Philosophy of Man,* offered additional insight. He wrote: "In Texas, years ago, almost all of the oil came from surface operations. Then

*Few people during their lifetime come anywhere near exhausting the resources dwelling within them. There are deep wells of strength that are never used.*

REAR ADMIRAL RICHARD BYRD

someone got the idea that there were greater sources of supply deeper down. A well was drilled five thousand feet deep. The result? A gusher. Too many of us operate on the surface. We never go deep enough to find the supernatural resources. The result is, we never operate at our best. More time and investment is (*sic*) involved to go deep but a gusher will pay off."

How deep have you dug? How long have you been dependent on surface abilities and talents? Have you tapped your inner supply of energy and potential? Are you satisfied with being an underachiever rather than being committed to maximum achieving? Have you become complacent, doing the same things, in the same way, with the same people, every day? In other words, are you going to get any better, or is this as good as it gets?

Successful and unsuccessful people do not vary significantly in what they are capable of doing. There is a giant chasm between successful and unsuccessful people in their desire to stretch and reach toward their potential. Brian Tracy believes, "Your remarkable and unusual combination of education, experience, knowledge, problems, successes, difficulties, and challenges, and your way of looking at and reacting to life, make you extraordinary. You have within you potential competencies and attributes that can enable you to accomplish virtually anything you want in life. Your main job is to decide which of your talents you're going to exploit and develop to their highest and best possible use right now."

**DIGGING DEEPER DEVICES**

**1. Think at a higher level.** Og Mandino observed, "Your only limitations are those you set up in your mind, or permit others to set up for you." Norman Vincent Peale believed, "You are greater than you think you are."

Digging deep toward your inner potential means expanding your mental boundaries. If you keep plowing around what appears to be mental obstacles, you'll never discover potential wealth below the surface. Think beyond present constraints. You must learn to see what isn't immediately evident. Don't limit your capabilities by what you currently see. Give yourself permission to dig to the next level. What you discover will determine what gets accomplished. Each time you determine, in the privacy of your mind, to cast aside limitations, your capacity to grow and perform dramatically expands.

Bible scholar C.I. Scofield reflected on a visit he made to a psychiatric hospital in Staunton, Virginia. The tour guide pointed out a powerfully built young man who seemed to be a picture of health.

Scofield asked, "Wouldn't that man be very difficult to manage if he became violent?" "Yes," said the guide, "but he never exerts his power. His delusion is that he has no strength! He is always asking for medicine and complaining of weakness."

The person you think you are is the person you will be.

**2. Perform at a higher level.** My hunting enthusiast friends tell me there is much to learn from ducks. There are two kinds of ducks: puddle ducks and divers. Puddle ducks such as Mallards, Redheads, and Mud Hens find pleasure in paddling around the edges of ponds, marshes, and lakes. They feed in shallow waters and eat only what they can reach from the surface. Diver ducks, on the other hand, are able to dive to incredible depths in a lake to feed from the plants at the bottom. Mergansers and Canvasbacks are representative of this group. Some divers can go to depths of 150 feet for their food.

Listening to my hunter friends talk of puddle ducks and divers reminded me of a direct correlation to the different types of people. There are people who are consistently satisfied with experiences, achievements, and nourishment found in easy tasks and just being good enough at what they do. Diver people go out on a limb. They look for adventurous opportunities to test their limits and pursue situations that will not only tap but enhance their potential.

Sounds simple, doesn't it? Becoming the best you can be means continually raising the performance bar. Rather than working within a restricting zone of comfort, a concentrated effort is needed to rise above your present level of performance. Demand more of yourself. Push yourself to perform beyond the obvious minimal expectations.

What do you currently do well? How frequently are you doing it? Are you getting better at it? How can you get more out of yourself? How deep are you diving within yourself to explore and experience new-found personal resources?

**3. Position yourself for a deep dig.** Psychologist Abraham Maslow determined that optimal mental health had seven requirements: (1) Take responsibility for your own feelings, including your own happiness; (2) Give up the luxury of blaming others for your shortcomings, disappointments, and suffering; (3) Face the consequences, even when the things you attempt and the risks you take bring about the worst possible results; (4) Seek to discover all the inner resources that are available to you, even though self-discovery is at times painful and demanding; (5) Act on your own feelings, rather than on the approval of others—even if this means conflict at times with those who are important to you; (6) Take responsibility for letting go of your own negativity, including letting yourself and other people off the hook; and (7) Have compassion and empathy for yourself and for others, recognizing that having compassion is a very healing process.

Maslow's mental health prerequisites set you up for optimal performance. They eliminate boundaries and excuses, putting you in the driver's seat to capitalize on possibilities.

No matter how you define success, regardless of how proud you are of your achievement, you have only discovered a minute portion of all you are capable of doing. You've barely scratched the surface and owe it to yourself to dig a little deeper. You can attain a different level of success. You certainly need not settle for the way things are. There is more in you than what you've already accomplished.

Look for, plan, expect, and act to create a breakthrough experience. "Knowing is not enough, we must apply. Willing is not enough, we must do," wrote the German philosopher Goethe. Far too few people act on their dreams, goals, and ambitions, and therefore restrict ongoing success. The more you activate the digging devices, the more results you'll discover.

At the height of her acting success, Barbra Streisand decided to produce and direct the movie *Yentl*. "Why on earth would you do such a thing," friends asked her. "It had nothing to do with the desire for fame and fortune," she responded. "I had all that. I did it because one night I dreamt that I had died, and God revealed my true potential to me. He told me about all the things I could have done, but didn't because I was afraid. That was when I decided that I had to create *Yentl* even if it cost me everything I had."

Streisand decided to dig a little deeper. So can you.

*He who would learn to fly one day must first learn to stand and walk and run and climb and dance; one cannot fly into flying.*

FRIEDRICH W. NIETZSCHE

❋

# THE ANCHOR
# OF ATTITUDE

❋

*Real optimism is aware of problems but
recognizes the solutions, knows about
difficulties but believes they can be
overcome, sees the negatives but
accentuates the positives, is exposed
to the worst but expects the best, has
reason to complain but chooses to smile.*

WILLIAM ARTHUR WARD

## MAKE EVERY HOUR
## A HAPPY HOUR

Have you ever been around people who are members of the Ain't-Life-Awful club? They are such a joy with which to associate! Their conversations consist of complaining about what a cruel world we live in, gossiping about the inadequacies of others, voicing how unappreciated they feel, and sharing how the circumstances in their life are unfair. Club members are even known to leave work at the end of the day and gather for "happy hour" from 5:00–7:00 to discuss how unhappy they are.

*The winner's edge is not in a gifted birth, a high IQ, or in talent. The winner's edge is all in the attitude, not aptitude. Attitude is the criterion for success.*

DENIS
WAITLEY

There is only one thing worse than being around people like this: It's *being* one of those people.

"Attitude is the first quality that marks the successful man," Lowell Peacock suggested. "If he has a positive attitude and is a positive thinker, who likes challenges and difficult situations, then he has half his success achieved." Your attitude, the way you see your world, determines the way you live, and your actions determine your accomplishment. Simply put, who you are today is a result of your attitude.

In his book *The Winning Attitude,* author and speaker John C. Maxwell says that attitude:

- is the "advance man" of our true selves
- has inward roots but outward fruits
- is our best friend or our worst enemy
- is more honest and more consistent than our words
- is an outward look based on past experiences
- is a thing which draws people to us or repels them
- is never content until it is expressed
- is the librarian of our past
- is the speaker of our present
- is the prophet of our future

Attitude may not be the only variable that determines your level of success, but it is certainly a primary contributor. One of the most significant attitudinal factors affecting your life is your expectation of life. Norman Vincent Peale preached, "The person who sends out positive thoughts activates the world around him positively and draws back to himself positive results."

You can learn to be more positive. There is no need to be saddled with the disheartening, deflating habit of seeing the dark side of life. If you're interested in creating an ongoing "happy hour," be assured there is only one person who can make it happen.

Begin by blocking out negativity. Stop yourself when you begin moaning, groaning, or complaining. Condition yourself to always search for the bright side of every situation. Run like crazy from negative, energy-draining people. Befriend co-workers who encourage others and display a spirit of gratitude. Focus on the present. Let go of past failures. Calm your anxiety about the future by expecting the best of today.

Before you can achieve the life you want, you must think, act, walk, talk, and behave in a way that exemplifies who you want to become. Don't expect an immediate transformation. Be patient with yourself. Lifestyle changes take time, but the result is worth the effort and wait.

DO WHAT YOU LOVE AND
SUCCESS WILL FOLLOW

*The talent of*
*success is*
*nothing more*
*than doing*
*what you can*
*do well; and*
*doing well*
*whatever you*
*do, without*
*the thought*
*of fame.*

HENRY
WADSWORTH
LONGFELLOW

❋

I've had the opportunity to encounter and observe a few people, who have quietly attained success without the fanfare or recognition of a fan club or fame. As I've watched their daily behavior, it has become evident that success is the result of the continual process of them becoming who they already were and loving what they do. No pretenses, no uncharacteristic behaviors, no facades; just a revealing of true character.

A fundamental characteristic of successful people is their ability to find out what they are good at and do it with a passion regardless of whether or not anyone else notices. Curtis Carlson advises, "You must listen to your own heart. You can't be successful if you aren't happy with what you're doing." The key here is being involved in something that utilizes your natural abilities. I can think of nothing worse than attempting to motivate myself in a position or activity that does not compliment my talents.

Michael Korda said, "Your chances of success are directly proportional to the degree of pleasure you derive from what you do. If you are in a job you hate, face the fact squarely and get out." As the old saying goes, "If the horse is dead, dismount." I don't think it's possible to ascend any further than what you are without first making sure that where you are is where you want to be.

Before jumping overboard, however, consider this. If you have a job that fails to stimulate, fulfill, and energize you, maybe there is a simple solution. How about changing your attitude about your job? Maybe you don't have to dismount. Could it be possible that changing how you view your life could ignite a new flame?

Whit Hobbs wrote, "Success is waking up in the morning, whoever you are, wherever you are, however old or young, and bounding out of bed because there's something out there that you love to do, that you believe in, that you're good at—something that's bigger than you are, and you can hardly wait to get at it again today."

Approaching everything you do with that upbeat attitude is bound to result in success.

*Career is too pompous a word. It was a job, and I have always felt privileged to be paid for what I am doing.*

BARBARA STANWYCK

## CAREER-GUIDING
## PRINCIPLES

If you were to leave your job today, what legacy would you leave? St. Augustine once said that adulthood begins when a person asks himself the question, "What do I want to be remembered for?" Have you begun your adulthood? Do you have any idea what affect you are making on those around you? Are there certain character traits, actions, or idiosyncrasies that will immediately make people think of you?

An unknown writer once communicated, "Methods are many; principles are few. Methods always change; principles never do." Principles are heart issues. It's difficult to communicate in written word the emotion that ignites these motivating forces. Nevertheless, here are the unchangeable principles that have guided, formed, and directed my life the past 20 years.

**1. My attitude about life will determine my quality of life.** Circumstances rarely dictate performance, but my perception of those events has dramatically affected my ability to deal with them. I figure there are two ways of approaching life: Either alter the circumstances, or alter yourself to meet them. What really matters is not the way things are, but the way you think things are, and how you decide to respond. John Maxwell is convinced that, "What I believe about life determines how I perceive life, which determines what I receive from life."

Your perception of and reaction to life's events will determine the affect they have on you. Every incident is merely an event waiting for you to develop an opinion about it. The attitude I display in life is a reflection of my internal beliefs, assumptions, and values. "You and I do not see things as they are," says Herb Cohen. "We see things as we are."

This is more than positive thinking. It is a process of making a conscious decision about what you will dwell on and how you will interpret any given situation.

**2. There is a miniscule difference between success and failure.** Success begins on the inside. NBA legend Michael Jordan said, "Heart is what separates the good from the great." Newsman Walter Cronkite declared, "I can't imagine a person becoming a success who doesn't give this game of life everything he's got."

The late Billy Martin was a controversial manager for the New York Yankees and established nonnegotiable standards for his players to follow. He let players know in no uncertain terms, "If you play for me, you play the game like you play life. You play it to be successful, you play it with dignity, you play it with pride, you play it aggressively, and you play it as well as you possibly can."

Are you getting the picture here? Successful people do a little more, raise the performance bar a little higher, expect higher results, and stick it out when things aren't going exactly as planned. Successful people invest 110 percent of themselves in their relationships. They continually monitor their attitude and make sure their energies are directed at their top priorities. They understand the need for total commitment to the task at hand and are determined to see it through to successful completion. Successful people are involved in a lifelong process of skill and competency development. They're not afraid to stand out from the crowd. In fact, they rather enjoy it.

Successful people do what's expected . . . and a little bit more. After Dallas won the Super Bowl in 1993, coach Jimmy Johnson commented, "I played for a national championship team, I coached a national championship team, and I coached a Super Bowl team. There's a common thread in all three: quality people who are committed to do their best." It's the miniscule difference between success and failure.

**3. Personal growth precedes personal fulfillment.** Bruce Springsteen believes, "A time comes when you need to stop waiting for the man you want to become and start being the man you want to be." You will never become what you ought to be until you begin doing what you ought to be doing to become what you want to be. Feeling good about your life is preceded by a willingness to learn, grow, and produce beyond your current accomplishments.

Sad is the day when people become content with their life, what they think, and the results they are producing. A multitude of opportunities await us every day to expand. Failure to pursue those windows of possibility will leave us unfulfilled and dissatisfied with life. It's not life's fault. Revitalize your life with a renewed commitment to a dream, results, and desire to tap into your potential achievement.

"If you're not doing something with your life," began a Peace Corps commercial, "it doesn't matter how long it is."

Life becomes boring when you stop growing and stretching. You become boring.

**4. When I help others to be successful, I will be successful.** The most successful people in the world are those who help other people become better and achieve more than they ever thought they could. Alan Lay McGinnis put it this way: "There is no more noble occupation in the world than to assist another human being—to help someone succeed."

I'm often asked what I mean by "helping someone succeed." Accept people with all of their irritating habits and idiosyncrasies—you have them, too. Always expect and discover the best in people. Listen without judgment and look them in the eye when they are talking. Pray for people. Share your affection. Laugh with people and cry with them as well. Send notes of encouragement and appreciation. Refrain from jealousy and anger. Celebrate people's successes with them. Go out of your way to be kind. Eliminate all ill will. Learn what is important to people and stand side by side with them in achieving their goals. Be a stimulant. Get excited about other people's lives and make it a point to help every person you work, live, or socialize with to feel important.

Joann C. Jones, writing in *Guideposts,* relayed the following story. "During my second year of nursing school our professor gave us a pop quiz. I breezed through the questions until I read the last one: 'What is the first name of the woman who cleans the school?'

"Surely this was some kind of joke. I had seen the cleaning woman several times, but how would I know her name? I handed in my paper, leaving the last question blank.

"Before the class ended, one student asked if the last question would count toward the grade. 'Absolutely,' the professor said. 'In your careers you will meet many people. All are significant. They deserve your attention and care, even if all you do is smile and say hello.'

"I've never forgotten that lesson. I also learned her name was Dorothy."

Helping others succeed is a simple, yet profound process of continually finding ways to enrich people's lives. From simply knowing their name, to walking step by step, side by side toward their dreams, your life will be filled with a multitude of moments to make a difference.

**5. Walk the talk.** St. Francis of Assisi once wisely said: "Preach the gospel at all times. If necessary, use words." We get so busy in the activities of life, we forget above all else what our life is communicating to others. Personality, work ethic, achievements, and our interactions with people display our good intentions. Who we are is the message. "So live that you wouldn't be ashamed to sell the family parrot to the town gossip," advised Will Rogers.

In his book with Ken Blanchard, *Everyone's a Coach,* Don Shula tells of losing his temper near an open microphone during a televised game with the Los Angeles Rams. Millions of viewers expressed surprise and shock by Shula's profanity. Letters arrived from all over the country, voicing their dissatisfaction and disbelief that this man of integrity could display such behavior.

Shula could have been tempted to offer excuses, but he didn't. Everyone who included a return address received a personal apology. He closed each letter by stating, "I value your respect and will do my best to earn it again."

Walking the talk doesn't mean living without mistakes but it does mean you are accountable for your behavior. Zig Ziglar was right. "Integrity," he says, "demands that you do the right thing so that you have fewer things to apologize for, explain away, or regret. Instead, cut your losses as quickly as possible after making a poor decision." Be quick to apologize when you fail to live up to the standards for which you hold yourself accountable.

Mark Twain knew how difficult it was to live an exemplary life. He once observed, "To do right is wonderful. To teach others to do right is even more wonderful—and much easier."

**6. Take responsibility for your life.** Never allow someone else or something outside of your control prevent you from succeeding. Give up all excuses, the blame game, and finger-pointing. "Success on any major scale requires you to accept responsibility," advises Michael Korda, editor-in-chief of Simon & Schuster. "In the final analysis, the one quality that all successful people have is the ability to take on responsibility."

You are completely responsible for what you do. Bern Williams has identified our modern-day unwillingness to take responsibility by speculating, "If Adam and Eve were alive today, they would probably sue the snake." We might chuckle at his suggestion, but I fear it is closer to the truth than most of us care to admit.

Responsibility is dreaded by many, but it is one choice that will make a substantial difference in changing your life. If you want to be happy with the life you live, get in charge. Take responsibility for where you are and where you're going. You are accountable for the results. You always have been and always will be. That's probably why Ed Cole suggested, "Maturity doesn't come with age; it comes with acceptance of responsibility."

Here's why this principle is so important. If you don't accept responsibility, you will soon identify yourself as a victim, and victims lead lives full of frustration, rationalization, blame, defensiveness, and excuses. I've cherished two questions that guard me from the snare of victimization. First, what do I want? Second, what am I willing to do to make it happen? The responsibility is on one person—me.

**7. Be willing to pay the price.** I've observed two kinds of people: those who get things done and those who wait for all the conditions to be just right before attempting anything. There are those who do whatever it takes and those who continually protest, "That's not my job." Zig Ziglar recommends, "If you do the things you need to do when you need to do them, the day will come when you can do the things you want to do when you want to do them."

Achievement is the result of doing what needs to be done, whether or not you feel like doing them. Don't wait to feel good before doing good. Pay the price now and experience the satisfaction of defying those little voices that tell you you're just not up to the task right now. "To achieve success, whatever the job we have, we must pay a price for success," said Vince Lombardi. "You have to pay the price to win and you have to pay the price to get to the point where success is possible. Most important, you must pay the price to stay there."

Legendary UCLA basketball coach John Wooden epitomized this principle. He never took success for granted. He knew there was a price to be paid each year, and resting on last year's success was not acceptable. He prepared his teams for battle. The continual development of skills, attitudes, teamwork, and a championship mindset produced phenomenal results. Wooden was so focused that he even required players to put on their socks a certain way, replace the soap in the shower stalls, and stack their dirty towels.

Ironically, as meticulous as Wooden was, he never relied on scouting reports or playbooks. He didn't want his players worrying about the opponent's weaknesses or strengths. He found playbooks useless because in the heat of the game, he knew he would need to make adjustments that couldn't be precalculated or written into a book of standard plays.

When you pay the price day in and day out, no matter how tedious or demanding it might seem, you will be rewarded with a champion lifestyle.

**8. Live to give.** "The measure of a life, after all, is not its duration but its donation," said Corrie Ten Boom. Generosity is a marvelous quality.

In our society, money tends to be the measuring stick for giving. What was her salary increase last year? How big was his performance bonus? What did that new car cost him? What was the increase in the bottom line? Our culture is obsessed with what people get.

Living to give involves so much more. The grave of Christopher Chapman in Westminster Abbey, bearing the date 1680, reads: *What I gave, I have; What I spent, I had; What I left, I lost; By not giving it.*

It's difficult to convince selfish people to begin giving of their resources, time, and talent. Sometimes it's easiest to write a check and hope nothing more is required. Step out by sharing thoughtfulness, sensitivity, and kindness with those needing a bit of compassion. Never turn your head on a co-worker needing to feel included.

Help someone who cannot help you in return. Encourage those who cannot help themselves. Nurture someone in moving toward his or her potential. Create a generous heart and heaven will be filled with people cheering when you get there.

**9. Live every day to the fullest.** "If you let yourself be absorbed completely," suggested Anne Morrow Lindbergh, "if you surrender completely to the moments as they pass, you live more richly in those moments."

This is such a simple principle for living, I am almost embarrassed to include it in the list. Yet, it seems people are always preparing to live. Someday they'll enjoy their job. Someday they'll have time for those they love. Someday they'll get actively involved in the adventure of living. What are they waiting for? Someday may never come.

Life isn't a dress rehearsal for the main event. You are living the main event. Look at your calendar for the week. Are there appointments, things on your to-do list, or responsibilities you dread? Decide you will meet them with a renewed passion. Look for little blessings in every corner of your life. Capture the miracle of life by giving each moment you live your best. Live every minute of every day to the fullest. Who knows, it might be your last.

"Seize the moment," encouraged Erma Bombeck. "Remember all those women on the *Titanic* who waved off the dessert cart."

**10. Keep success in perspective.** Singer Jon Bon Jovi's parents told him he could achieve anything, so he worked tirelessly on his musical career from the time he was 16. His band became phenomenally successful, but Jon Bon Jovi hit the wall and realized there had to be more to life than the reckless pace, physical exhaustion, or continual pressure to produce another No. 1 album or No. 1 single. His wife, Dorothea, gave him the room and encouragement to put it all in perspective.

"Today," says Bon Jovi, "I try to spend as much time on my marriage and parenting as I do on my career. For years we had a funny adage in our house that was, 'It's about me, me, me, the singer.' Now it's no longer about me, it's about them. We stay home, making sure the kids have a healthy, loving environment."

Success is all about recognizing and appreciating the love and respect of those closest to you. What good is success if the people around you are being hurt in the process? What good is success if it is not contributing to the long-term health and benefit of those you love? What good is success if you don't have someone you love to share it with?

As much as I enjoy the pursuit of dreams, goals, and accomplishments, the long-term value is small compared with the privilege of savoring each day with those I love and respect.

That's it. The ten principles that guide my life are simple, but they've been effective in providing a compass for my personal and professional pursuits. How about you? Have you decided what unwavering, unchangeable principles will direct your life?

# BUILD A
# BETTER YOU

*Character is what we do when no one is looking. It is not the same as reputation . . . success . . . achievement. Character is not what we have done, but who we are.*

BILL HYBELS

## PAY ATTENTION TO
## WHO YOU ARE

John Luther once said, "Good character is more to be praised than outstanding talent. Most talents are, to some extent, a gift. Good character, by contrast, is not given to us. We have to build it piece by piece—by thought, choice, courage, and determination." Character has to do with how people are put together. It's the interaction between what they believe and what they do. Although talent is important to be successful in your job, character is imperative.

In his book *Everything You've Heard Is Wrong,* Tony Campolo tells this great story. Once upon a time there was an office manager who lost his job during the recession. In his sadness he wandered into a park, found himself an empty bench, and sat down. After a while another man came strolling along. This second man was especially sad as he took a seat at the opposite end of the bench.

*Hard work spotlights the character of people: some turn up their sleeves, some turn up their noses, and some don't turn up at all.*

SAM EWING

After these two men had sat silently for a couple of hours, the first man said, "I'm an office manager who has been made redundant. I don't have a job anymore. What's your problem?"

The second man answered, "I own a circus. The big attraction at my circus was an ape. Last week the ape died, and the crowds have fallen off to almost nothing. I think I'm going to be out of business if I don't find another ape."

It did not take long for the first man to come up with an interesting proposal. "You need an ape and I need a job. What if I dress up in the ape's skin and pretend to be real? I could carry on for your patrons and everybody would be happy."

Having nothing to lose, the circus owner decided to give it a try. To his surprise the fake ape proved to be more exciting and drew larger crowds than the real one had. Money came pouring in, and both the former office manager and the circus owner were getting rich.

Then, one day, things got out of hand. Somehow a lion got into the same cage with the fake ape. The office manager didn't know what to do. He maneuvered as best he could to escape the claws of the lion but realized that sooner or later he would be a "goner."

A large crowd gathered outside the cage to watch the spectacle. They screamed and gasped as the lion finally trapped the office manager in a corner of the cage and poised himself to leap on the make-believe ape. Suddenly, the shocked crowd heard the ape yell in a shaken, frightened voice, "Help! Help!"

It was then that the lion muttered under his breath, "Shut up, stupid! Do you think you're the only one around here that's out of a job?"

It's amazing how many people are walking around pretending to be something they aren't. They invest substantial energy creating an identity that will be acceptable to those around them. The problem is, they find it necessary to keep changing their public appearance to meet the vacillating expectations of the people they are with. It's impossible to play this game for a lifetime. Sooner or later, they get cornered and the "real person" is exposed.

Career success is grounded in behavior that is consistent with the values we espouse. Violating personal values is harmful to the person as well as the organization. Pretending leads to personal sabotage and self-protective behaviors. I would have to agree with John Morley, who observed, "No man can climb out beyond the limitations of his own character." When your character is strong, people trust you to perform up to your potential. When character is questionable, people never know what to expect.

Be a professional who knows what's right and does it, even if it means putting forth substantially more effort. Doing what's easy or convenient isn't necessarily consistent with what's right.

Let your commitment to values drive your actions. Is it risk free? Will it be well received? Am I in the mood to do it? These are not the questions values-driven people ask. Are my behaviors in line with my ethical commitment? Do I believe in what I'm doing? Am I maintaining my integrity with this decision? These are the questions that surface when character is in charge.

Maintain the highest standards. Your character comes to life through your values, integrity, and honesty . . . the consistency between your words and actions. Understand that your convictions might not initially win a popularity contest, especially if they violate "the way we've always done it." Remind yourself that the right things are not always rewarded and not everybody will be on your side.

Take full responsibility for your character. "Everybody's doing it" is juvenile and doesn't cut it. You can't put someone else in charge of your ethics. Try it, and you'll soon find yourself lowering your standards. "I'm just doing what I'm told" is a cop out. Character is a personal decision and quest. Your beliefs might coincide with the people you work with, but ultimately character is an individual exercise.

Character-driven people are willing to do the things emotion-driven people will not do. They take pride in their dependability, commitment to excellence, willingness to serve others, solution-minded approach to problems and their internal drive . . . regardless of how they "feel." This isn't a sometime thing or a 90-percent thing; either you have it or you don't. Even brief leaks can be devastating.

According to a 1997 *USA Today* article, scientists are now convinced that a series of slits, not a gash, sank the *Titanic*.

As the extremely successful movie reminded us, the 900-foot unsinkable cruise ship sank in 1912 on its first voyage, from England to New York. Fifteen hundred people met a tragic death in this ocean disaster.

The widely held belief that the ship hit an iceberg, resulting in a huge gash in the side of the liner, is now in question. An international team of divers and scientists used sound waves to probe the wreckage, resting in mud two-and-a-half miles deep. They were shocked to find the damage to the ship was relatively small. Instead of a huge gash, they discovered six relatively narrow slits across the six water-tight holds.

What an incredible find! Six small leaks caused the demise of a giant, steel vessel. Likewise, small leaks, insignificant compromises, undefined parameters, and ignored values can sink a person's character. Pay attention to who you are. It's more than a reputation. Reputation is what you are supposed to be. Character is what you are.

Like the *Titanic,* a reputation doesn't mean much unless it can stand up under a lifetime of pressure. Be encouraged by the words of Bobby Richardson who said, "Any man will command respect if he takes a stand and backs it up with his life."

GET A BETTER VIEW
OF YOURSELF

*Doubt yourself
and you doubt
everything you
see. Judge
yourself and
you see judges
everywhere. But
if you listen to
the sound of
your own voice,
you can rise
above doubt and
judgment, and
you can see
forever.*

NANCY
KERRIGAN

❋

From *Sunday Sermons* comes the story of a man who brought his boss home for dinner for the first time. The boss was very blustery, very arrogant, very dominating! The little boy in the family stared at his father's boss for most of the evening, but did not say anything. Finally, the boss asked the little boy, "Why do you keep looking at me like that, Sonny?" The little boy answered, "My daddy says you are a self-made man." The boss beamed and proudly admitted that indeed he was a self-made man. The little boy said, "Well, if you are a self-made man, why did you make yourself like that?"

This little story prompts a chuckle every time I think about it. The little boy's comment also creates a few sobering thoughts. We all have our own struggles with becoming the person we want to be. There may be times we even ask ourselves: "Why did I make myself like this?"

During one of my seminars, I often ask the question, "How many of you believe in yourself 100 percent?" Rarely does a hand go up. As I work my way down the percentage scale, the majority of hands are raised somewhere between 50 and 75 percent. Two important questions are then posed to the group: (1) What keeps you from achieving 100 percent, and (2) What would your work place be like if everyone believed in themselves 100 percent?

Believing in yourself 100 percent does not equate with arrogance, pride, or conceit. It's the maximum utilization of the gifts, abilities, and talents you've been given. On the flip side, believing in yourself halfway will not provide the motivation necessary to go beyond where you are.

Much of our insecurity about ourselves on the job is prompted by feeling we're not so good as other people and there's little chance things are going to get any better. To break out of this thinking, we need to reform our current beliefs and begin questioning the assumptions we make about ourselves.

Breaking through cemented images we have of ourselves is no easy task. Begin by seeing the person you want to become and then work backwards to make that image a reality. My friend Joe Batten says, "When you know who and what we wish to be, we will find it relatively easy to know what to do." Begin acting like the person you want to become. Portray the confidence that person will have. Behave as if you are already that person. As you begin getting a better view of yourself, keep a few things in mind.

**Be yourself.** Brian Tracy believes, "The world will largely accept you at your own estimation. It is yourself that you have to convince before you can convince anyone else."

Willy Loman, in the powerful, yet tragic play, *Death of a Salesman,* lived a life filled with phony clichés. Willy struggled to discover who he really was and because of this lived a life of fear, doubt, and insecurity. *Death of a Salesman* recently experienced a surge in popularity. I can't help but wonder if Willy Loman is more than a character for those who attend the play. Could it be he portrays a world full of people trying to be like, act like, and succeed like other people? "So much restlessness," suggests Lin Yutang, "is due to the fact that one does not know what one wants, or wants too many things, or perhaps wants to be somebody else; to be anybody except one's self. There is courage in being one's genuine self, or standing alone and not wanting to be somebody else."

Theologian Charles Spurgeon warned, "Beware of no one more than yourself; we carry our worst enemies within us." It's important to discover who you really are—your character, values, and heart—before you attempt to build on what you have. "Human being" does indeed precede "human doing."

**Be genuine.** Unfortunately, Ava Gardner represented a lot of people when she said, "Deep down, I'm pretty superficial."

The best way to describe what I mean by being genuine is to share an illustration that is totally contrary to what I mean. In the October 26, 1992 issue of *The New York Times,* an article headlined "Fragrance Engineers Say They Can Bottle the Smell of Success," by N.R. Kleinfield, begins like this:

"It was bound to happen. Someone thinks he is about to create the Honest Car Salesman in a bottle.

"A year ago, one of Detroit's Big Three auto makers hired Dr. Alan R. Hirsch, a quirky smell researcher in Chicago, to devise a rather exceptional scent. The hope was that when the odor was sprayed on a car salesman, he would—yes—smell honest.

"It sounds absurd. In fact, after she was done laughing, Dr. Susan Shiffman, a smell researcher and professor of medical psychology at the Duke University Medical School, remarked, 'I was not aware that honesty had a specific smell associated with it.' But Dr. Hirsch, who refuses to name his Detroit client, is confident that he will have the Honest Car Salesman Odor devised within a year. If he succeeds, he said, the auto maker will entrust the smell to its dealers, who will spray it on their salesmen, and then customers will catch a whiff and cars will fly off the lots."

Believe it or not, this is a true story. My response is, "If you're trying to cover up a character flaw with a scented spray, don't expect to achieve a respectable reputation or increased self respect." Norman Vincent Peale once said, "It is a fact that you project what you are." Be genuine. Phonies ultimately end up disliking themselves.

**Be assured you are somebody special.** According to *Parade,* the 1992 November ballot in the state of Washington carried a candidate named "Absolutely Nobody." David Powers had his name legally changed to capitalize on voter frustration and promised to abolish the office of Lieutenant Governor if elected. He lost with 6 percent of the vote, but what if he had won? "Absolutely Nobody Wins!"

How true! People who believe they are nobody never win. They might get attention or even sympathy, but it's short lived and they end with a small percent of support, leaving them worse off than they were before. "My advice is, follow my advice," advises Miss Piggy. "Never forget that only you can ever fully appreciate your own true beauty. Others may try, but they so often fall short." Louis L'Amour said it a little differently, "I am somebody. I am me. I like being me. And I need nobody to make me somebody." Being somebody special begins with believing you are somebody special. See your own goodness, appreciate your assets, and celebrate your humanness.

In addition, Denis Waitley suggests, "Faith in yourself begins with understanding that God is always with you and within you." Waitley's comment is comforting. God is bigger than any limitation you possess and capable of turning your greatest weakness into a strength.

There is a story told by entertainer Roger Williams that has some relevance here. It seems the famous singer was on tour and stopped by a nursing home to visit his mother. He said he got lost looking for her room and was wandering around somewhat confused when an elderly woman came up to him and looked at him with an intensely curious, but recognizing stare. After a moment, he awkwardly broke the silence asking, "Do you know who I am?"

*You are free to choose where you work, what you do, and with whom you will work. But who and what you become is hanging in the balance. Before you take a job or position, remind yourself that what will go on in the workplace will change you, and ask yourself whether or not the change will be in harmony with your mission statement.*

TONY
CAMPOLO

❋

Surveying him from head to toes, she replied, "No, but if you go to the front desk, they can tell you."

We don't need someone else telling us who we are, but to increase our value to the company, our co-workers and customers, knowing who we are and striving to be what we want to become is important. Dr. Joyce Brothers reminds us, "You cannot consistently perform in a manner which is inconsistent with the way you see yourself." Therefore, staying neutral is not an option. We need to move forward to discipline ourselves toward positive, constructive action that moves us continually in the direction of becoming all we can be. That's how you get a better view of yourself.

## BE THE BEST YOU
## CAN BE

John C. Maxwell, writing in *Developing the Leader Within You,* says, "Most people have a desire to look at the exception instead of the desire to become the exceptional." The reality is, it takes a ton of effort to become exceptional and very little effort to find excuses for why we aren't performing at our best. There is a personal price to pay to excel in your career. No shortcuts are available.

"Excellence," says Pat Riley, "is the gradual result of always striving to do better." Notice Riley didn't say, "If you do this one thing, you'll have mastered the formula for excellence." Reaching your optimum performance requires small steps to help you grow so you're prepared for your next level of performance. I've observed a number of practical strategies employed by people who realize and are motivated by the fact that "average" is as close to the bottom as it is to the top. They don't want to spend their career in that limbo position.

*If you want to achieve excellence, you can get there today. As of this second, quit doing less than excellent work.*

THOMAS WATSON

❃

Different things seem to work for different people. However, a few of the strategies are relatively universal. Consider the following approaches for planning your excursion away from average toward your peak performance.

**1. Fix the flaws.** Running back Rashaan Salaam's outstanding rushing career in college earned him the Heisman Trophy in 1995. He was drafted by the Chicago Bears, and although he led the Bears in rushing during the rookie season, opponents spotted a weakness in his game. Salaam was prone to fumble. In fact, he gave up the ball nine times.

According to the *Chicago Tribune,* the Chicago Bears's coaching staff devised a practical drill to correct the problem. They tied a long strap around a football. As Rashaan ran with the ball tightly clutched against his body, another player ran behind him yanking on the strap. Rashaan learned to squeeze the ball with such power that it could not be forced free.

People who are committed to excellence in their careers identify what top-notch performance would look like and then move towards that standard. As this process evolves, needed corrections unfold and adjustments are made to insure a steady progress toward the ideal. Minor flaws, imperfections, and less-than-desirable outcomes are bound to surface. That's a natural part of the process. What separates the excellent from the mediocre performers is the determination to correct faults that undermine their desire to be the best they can be. As Oliver Cromwell said in the early 17th century, "The person who stops being better, stops being good." It's a never-ending quest.

I'm not an advocate for investing massive attention and energy on fixing what's wrong and letting the strengths take care of themselves. Quite the contrary. Yet, you can't overlook those issues that keep you from scaling new heights, refining your expertise, or achieving expanded results. But just removing or correcting the weaknesses doesn't mean everything will be perfect. You might have an error-free day, but not necessarily one that could be defined as excellent. Rashaan Salaam may not fumble the ball during an entire game, but that doesn't mean he has a successful day in the backfield. More is needed than "just" managing our limitations or weaknesses.

**2. Find your sweet spot.** After decades of work as a consultant with major companies and a prolific writing career, Peter Drucker made this observation: "The great mystery isn't that people do things badly but that they occasionally do a few things well. The only thing that is universal is incompetence. However, nobody ever commented, for example, that the great violinist, Jascha Heifetz, probably couldn't play the trumpet very well."

Finding that niche, talent, or interest where excellence can be achieved is a great way to maximize your efforts. When we find that "sweet spot," as in tennis or golf, increased power and control are at our disposal.

As Alfred North Whitehead put it, "Doing little things well is the way toward doing big things better."

Capitalizing on your sweet spot keeps you reaching, stretching to perfect your skills and to outdo yesterday. You may see bit-by-bit improvement, but it's enough to eventually add up to a significant increase in your expertise. Use your sweet spots to trigger dramatic performance breakthroughs, protect your career, improve your value to the company, and prepare the way for a bright future. Think of it as a daily pursuit of perfection that will upgrade your contribution to the team and organization.

**3. Focus on doing your best.** While serving in the United States Navy, Jimmy Carter applied for the nuclear submarine program. Admiral Hyman Rickover was the head of the United States Nuclear Navy at the time, and everyone knew about his reputation for being a stern and demanding admiral. Jimmy Carter had to interview with the legendary admiral. Those who had endured past interviews knew that applicants usually came out in fear, anger, and totally intimidated. But, he was the door that had to be passed through.

Carter reflected that, for the first part of the interview, the admiral allowed him to talk about any topic he wanted to discuss. He chose subjects that were familiar to him, but by the time the admiral asked him increasingly difficult questions about the topic, Carter learned he knew relatively little about the subject.

Toward the end of the interview, the Admiral asked, "How did you stand in your class at the Naval Academy?" Carter proudly answered, "Sir, I stood fifty-ninth in a class of 820." He fully expected a hearty congratulations from the admiral, but instead received a surprising response. Rickover asked, "Did you do your best?"

Carter began to answer, "Yes, sir," but then took a moment to reflect on times when he could have learned more about America's allies and enemies, weapons, strategy, and the like. He finally responded, "No, sir, I didn't always do my best."

Admiral Rickover looked at Carter for a long time, turned his chair around to end the interview, and then threw one final question at his applicant. He said, "Why not?"

Was Admiral Rickover too harsh? Did he demand too much of a young seaman? Were his expectations unrealistic? Not according to Jimmy Carter. He said he never forgot Admiral Rickover's words to him that day. Years later, that encounter prompted a title for his book: *Why Not the Best?*

In an effort to keep up in this fast-paced world, some people lower their standards and expect less than excellence from themselves. Sacrifices are made in the name of efficiency. Unfortunately, such a move can reduce a person's performance to mediocrity. Colin Powell is right, "The freedom to be your best means nothing unless you're willing to do your best."

"Are you doing your best?" Raise your standards. Establish a baseline of which you can be proud. Make no exceptions. Instead of accepting less than your best, improve upon your personal best. "Aim at perfection in everything," suggested Lord Chesterfield, "though in most things, it is unattainable. However, they who aim at it, and persevere, will come much nearer to it than those whose laziness and despondency make them give it up as unattainable." Reach for new heights. Go above and beyond the call of duty. Do more than others expect. Never accept so-so performance in yourself or those around you.

This is a great time to be the best you can be . . . in everything . . . in every way.

*Over and over again mediocrity is promoted because real worth isn't to be found.*

KATHLEEN NORRIS

# MAKE THINGS
# HAPPEN

✺

*Nothing is so fatiguing as the eternal*
*hanging on of an uncompleted task.*

WILLIAM JAMES

## COMPLETE
## UNCOMPLETED TASKS

W hat do you remember most—the tasks you have completed or those you have yet to do? Most people immediately respond, "I remember most the things I have left to do."

I'm always challenged (and often embarrassed) when I arrive home at night and my wife asks, "What did you do today?" There are some days I must honestly respond, "I don't know for sure. But it took me all day to do it."

Failure to make significant progress completing work demands is a major source of frustration, stress, and disappointment. Only an obsession for completion can erase the negative results and feelings associated with loose ends.

Existing in a frantic whirlwind of commitments and activities is not the same as producing results. In fact, an estimated one-third of the American workforce doesn't accomplish what it sets out to do each day. Is it any wonder why we have a nation of unfulfilled workers?

*What you accomplish in life depends almost completely upon what you make yourself do. The very first thing one should do is to train the mind to concentrate upon the essentials and discard the frivolous and unimportant. This will assure real accomplish-ment and ultimate success.*
LYNDON
JOHNSON

Henry David Thoreau observed, "It's not enough to be industrious, so are the ants. What are you industrious about?"

What is your definition of work? Is it a series of activities and responsibilities? If so, then work is viewed as a verb. Everybody works, but not everybody is productive.

Productive people see work as what they are able to achieve. It is a noun. What evolves out of completed tasks is a feeling of being in control, increased productivity, heightened satisfaction, increased time for other responsibilities, and more energy to be creative. Until we develop a mindset that what we achieve is far more important than being busy, completing uncompleted tasks will not be a priority.

Review your pending assignments, the pile of unread journal articles, correspondence awaiting your reply, and the return phone calls you've been avoiding. Simplify your approach and plan to unclutter your life (and desk) by seeing these responsibilities through to completion.

Completion produces a satisfaction that the result has been achieved. You can mark it off your to-do list and get a fresh start. There's a new freedom to pursue the next priority. Creativity increases. Your energy tank will be refilled and you will be able to refocus attention. A renewed momentum is in place.

Look for ways to bring closure and completion to your daily assignments. We live in a time when working hard is not nearly so important as getting work done. You will be recognized and remembered for what you have done, not for how busy you were or how good your intentions were.

**Simple hint:** If you have difficulty bringing closure to your work, pretend you're going on vacation next week. I'm convinced a national survey would produce a phenomenal correlation between efficiency, effectiveness, results, and the timing of vacations.

HALF
FINISHED

*If you are wearing out the seat of your pants before you do your shoe soles, you're making too many contacts in the wrong place.*

ANONYMOUS

❀

Winter in the Midwest provides ample opportunity for any youngster with a little gumption to benefit from the lack of motivation displayed by others. After a heavy snowfall, we would grab our shovels and go in search of adults discouraged by nature's actions. Youthful ingenuity led us to people whose driveways were half finished. In fact, hearing someone say, "Can't you see I'm already half finished?" tickled our hearts. These people lost interest in their activity and would usually turn over their driveway (and their money) to our ambitions and willingness to finish what they had started.

Stick-to-itiveness is a quality lacking in the day-to-day affairs of many people. We can never be what we ought to be until we start doing what we ought to be doing. Then we need to continue doing what we ought to be doing so we can achieve what we are capable of achieving. "You will never stub your toe standing still," reflected Charles F. Kettering. "The faster you go, the more chance there is of stubbing your toe, but the more chance you have of getting somewhere."

Don't get bogged down in preparing to take action. Preparation is often a stall tactic, an excuse for fearing what your actions might produce or fail to produce. Very little can be accomplished unless you go ahead and do it before you're ready. When you hear someone constantly talking about what they are going to do tomorrow, rest assured they probably said the same thing yesterday.

A lifestyle of inactivity, procrastination, or quitting perpetuates itself. There is a cure. William James, the father of American psychology, suggested three rules for making things happen in life:

1. Start immediately.
2. Do it flamboyantly.
3. No exceptions.

Put another way, get up, get active, wear out your soles, and stick to it with unwavering tenacity. "To know what has to be done, and then do it," said Sir William Osler, "comprises the whole philosophy of practical life."

*Take time to deliberate; but when the time for action arrives, stop thinking and go in.*
ANDREW JACKSON

## FILL HOLES OR
## PLANT TREES

I love the story about a farmer sitting on his porch watching a highway department work crew. A worker got out of the truck, dug a good-sized hole in the ditch, and climbed back into the vehicle. A few minutes later, a pick-up truck pulled up as the first truck drove forward on the shoulder of the road. A worker stepped out of the pick-up, filled up the hole, tamped the dirt, and got back in his vehicle. The two-man work crew repeated the process—digging, waiting, refilling. After a few repetitions, the farmer made his way to the workers. "What are you doing?" he asked.

"We're on a beautification project," one worker responded, "and the guy who plants the trees is on vacation."

I like being around people who make things happen. Organizations need people who want to make a difference, not those who simply keep busy, like the beautification crew. These "busy" people keep filling holes without creating visible improvements or generating results. Call it busy work without productivity. These people are a dime a dozen.

On the other hand, co-workers who are excited about their responsibilities, recognize the importance of their role, apply themselves to the job at hand, and desire to improve the way things are achieve appreciable results. No matter how seemingly unimportant or insignificant their role, they keep moving forward, positioning themselves to perform on a higher plane.

Organizations need people willing to take initiative by making bold moves to advance the organization's effectiveness. There's plenty of room for people who constantly think of new ways to contribute to the team. Shattering the *status quo,* endorsing risk, and making gutsy moves to benefit the organization isn't written in their job descriptions. These are the unwritten qualifications that separate mediocre and successful people. As William Arthur Ward said, "Blessed is the person who sees the need, recognizes the responsibility, and actively becomes the answer."

Watching people who lack this type of initiative is frustrating. As they sit around waiting for further instructions or permission to act, a countless number of growth opportunities pass them by. It's as if they are orchestrating the death of their career.

Business giant Conrad Hilton suggested, "Success seems to be connected with action. Successful people keep moving. They make mistakes, but they don't quit." People who take audacious action may not always be right but it's proof they are interested in doing more than staying busy—filling a hole. Besides, they normally keep on investing themselves until they get things right. They crush through old habits and move beyond the routine of doing the same things, the same way, every day.

We live in a fast-paced, impatient world that rewards the person who approaches each task with a sense of urgency. The world won't wait around for those who wait to be perfect before taking action. Focused energy, in the face of uncertainty, is rewarded.

Make yourself more valuable. Emphasize action. Don't get bogged down in purposeless activity. Seek radical achievement. There is always a hole to be filled. Don't wait for someone else to plant the tree. Take the initiative. Very little will be accomplished unless you go ahead and do it. Others will follow.

In the words of Theodore Roosevelt, "Get action. Do things; be sane, don't fritter away your time; create, act, take a place wherever you are and be somebody. Get action."

*Four little words sum up what has lifted most successful individuals above the crowd: a little bit more. They did all that was expected of them and a little bit more.*

A. LOU
VICKERY

# SUCCESS IS
# WHERE YOU
# FIND IT

✳

*Remember, when you can, that the definition
of success has changed. It is not only survival,
the having—it is the quality of every moment
of your life, the being. Success is not a
destination, a place you can ever get to;
it is the quality of the journey.*

JENNIFER JAMES

*Success Is the Quality of the Journey*

DEVELOP YOUR PICTURE
OF SUCCESS

The topic of success often produces two dominant questions: What is success? How do you attain it? My journey to answer these questions and understand success has taken a number of twists and turns. The older I get, the more reflective I become on the subject and the less dogmatic I am about my observations. I have concluded that people need to determine for themselves what success will mean to them.

*A Thoroughbred horse never looks at the other horses. It just concentrates on running the fastest race it can.*

HENRY FONDA

For me, that person is a success who enjoys life, lives it to the fullest, and helps others do the same. Success is ultimately an individual feeling of fulfillment, satisfaction, and a desire to continue growing. John Maxwell defined success in *The Success Journey* as "Knowing my purpose in life, growing to maximum potential, and sowing seeds that benefit others." In your lifelong success journey, Maxwell suggests, "Two things are required for success: the right picture of success and the right principles for getting there."

What is the right picture of success? Real-estate magnate Donald Trump suggested, "The real measure of success is how happy you are. I have a lot of friends who don't have a lot of money, but they are a lot happier than I am, so therefore I say that they are probably more successful." That's a nice thought, but there are countless people who are always searching for something more to make them happy. In fact, I'm convinced some people are only happy when they're unhappy. Happiness can certainly be one of many by-products of success, but rarely a measure of success.

Many other so-called success guideposts lead to equally miserable results. The attainment of the ideal job, achieving financial security, landing a major account, completing a challenging project, or building the dream home are empty measurements of success. That's not to say these aren't honorable pursuits, but when used as success indicators, they will fall far short of being classified as enduring factors.

I tend to concur with football great Joe Kapp who said, "Success is living up to your potential. That's all. Wake up with a smile and go after life. . . . Live it, enjoy it, taste it, smell it, feel it." Equally powerful is Ralph Waldo Emerson's reflection, "Laugh often; to win the respect of intelligent people and the affection of children; to appreciate honest criticism and endure the betrayal of false friends; to find the best in others; to leave the world a bit better; to know even one life has breathed easier because you have lived—this is to have succeeded." Successful people understand that success isn't some distant destination or a final achievement, but a process of successful living.

There's probably no one picture of success that suits everybody. Ultimately, it's up to you to decide and define what success means to you. Don't get caught up in what society, your co-workers, friends, or even extended family think is the definition of success. The difficulty of attempting to live up to others' expectations can be exasperating. Success is a highly personal thing and by deciding what the picture of success looks like, you set the stage to understand and pursue the principles that will get you there.

According to a 1993 *Pryor Report,* executives from 200 of the nation's largest companies were asked, "Of successful people you have met over the years, which of the following is the main reason for their success: (a) contacts, (b) determination, (c) hard work, (d) knowledge, or (e) luck?" In response, 40 percent of these high-powered executives indicated success was due to hard work and 38 percent said determination. Seventy-eight percent attributed success to hard work and determination.

A combination of hard work and determination define Olympic gold-medalist Janet Evans. She became the only American woman to win an Olympic individual swimming event. Evans, as a 17-year-old high school senior, took Seoul, Korea by storm in the fall of 1988. This Olympic wonder didn't settle for just one medal; she won three: the 400-meter freestyle, the 800-meter freestyle, and the 400-meter individual medley. If that isn't enough, Evans shattered her own world record with a 4:03.85 clocking in the 400-meter freestyle.

How was this young, untested Olympic swimmer able to excel under constant attention, pressure, and media focus? For five years prior, beginning at age 12, Evans committed herself to a rigorous daily training schedule. She began the day at 4:45 A.M. with a four-mile swim, followed by school, then homework, and back to the pool for a 9,000-meter swim. Janet was home by 6:00 for supper, a bit more homework, and in bed by 8:00 P.M. to prepare her body for another demanding day. Hard work and determination enabled Janet Evans to become the winner of 45 U.S. National Titles and the holder of six American records.

"But wait," you might say, "I thought success and achievement were not synonymous." When you combine knowing where you are going, striving to become your personal best, and helping others to do the same, with the qualities of hard work and unwavering dedication, good things happen. Janet Evans meshed together her picture of success and the required effort to attain it. "Success," suggests Brian Tracy, "comes from doing what you are ideally suited to do, doing it extremely well, and doing more and more of it."

Once you determine what your picture of success will look like, you might find the following suggestions helpful to clarify the principles that will guide your journey.

Basketball great Michael Jordan offered this insight: "Success isn't something you chase. It's something you have to put forth the effort for constantly. Then maybe it'll come when you least expect it. Most people don't understand that."

Author and professional speaker Carl Mays suggests, "The whole business of finding success is to make the most of who you are, with what you have, where you are."

"No one ever attains very eminent success by simply doing what is required of him," said Charles Kendall. "It is the amount and excellence of what is over and above the required that determines greatness."

When a reporter asked Thomas Edison to what he attributed his success, he replied, "The ability to apply my physical and mental energies to one problem incessantly without growing weary is my secret to success."

Violinist Isaac Stern believed, "There should be at least three cardinal rules for success in personal achievement, whatever the field may be: (1) complete passionate devotion to whatever field you have chosen; (2) the need to concentrate, to the exclusion of all else, when working on, thinking about, or executing whatever discipline you have chosen; (3) an utter pitiless sense of self-criticism, far greater than that which any outsider could give."

Booker T. Washington shared this interesting slant: "Success is not measured by the position one has reached in life, rather by the obstacles overcome while trying to succeed."

There's a wealth of practical advice in these success tidbits. You might even be able to add your own profound insight. One common theme permeates everything we read, hear, or experience about success—people who enjoy successful moments in their life are not couch potatoes waiting for success to happen. Successful people understand that success is all about who you are, and what you are doing every moment of your life to cause good things to happen.

Don't complicate the issue of success. Develop a clear picture of what success will mean to you and then endeavor to do something every day that will make that picture a reality.

## WHAT IMPRESSION
## WOULD YOU HAVE MADE?

*You always do whatever you want to do. This is true of every act. Only you have the power to choose for yourself. The choice is yours. You hold the tiller. You can alter the course you choose in the direction of where you want to be—today, tomorrow, or in a distant time to come.*

W. CLEMENT
STONE

It's been quite a week. I've been flying in small commuter planes from one speaking engagement to another, sleeping in a variety of hotels, eating on the run, and attempting to be productive in airports. Although I immense-ly enjoyed every group I spoke to, I'm tired. Whenever I get tired, I get reflective.

Throughout the week I've strolled through airports observing uptight and stressed travelers. "What do you mean you can't deliver!" I overheard a sales person scream over the phone. "How could the flight leave without me?" demanded a frustrated vacationer. Countless people shuffled, ran, or slowly meandered through the airport hallways with a scowl on their face and pain in their eyes.

Two men, sitting near me on one flight, sounded like dueling banjos as they downgraded, bamblasted, and gener-ally ripped apart their companies. According to them, they weren't being paid enough, worked too many hours, and their bosses didn't have the slightest idea how difficult their jobs were. "Why in the world are they still on board?" I thought to myself.

Leonard, on the other hand, either loved his job at an airport coffee stand or he was preparing to audition for a professional acting career. His entertaining comments, happy feet, and friendly demeanor prompted me to increase the tip I had intended to give. I revisited him on my return through the airport later in the week. He was still there. Same song . . . second verse.

Bill loved his job as well. He told me so on our trip from the hotel to the airport. "Never thought I could enjoy work this much," this sixty-something courtesy van driver told me. He was genuinely interested in what I did for a living, had strong, positive feelings about his employer, and was well versed in the community and nation's current events. The 15-minute ride went far too fast. Bill gave courtesy drivers a *great* name.

Audrey also impressed me. She worked at the front desk of the Bismarck, North Dakota hotel where I was speaking. I had limited time after my seminar to get to the airport. I also needed to have the hotel send a box back to my office. Audrey immediately took charge, filled out the paperwork, weighed the box, smiled, and assured me she would personally take care of it. I extended my heartfelt thanks. "No problem," she responded, "that's what I'm here for." I like people like that!

Beau was equally impressive. He wore a seemingly permanently affixed massive smile across his face that only slightly diminished as he hoisted my heavy luggage into the van. "Is there somewhere we can stop on the way to the airport for a cup of gourmet coffee?" I asked. "You bet," he replied. He shared his passion for the theater and his aspirations to perform on stage. Beau had already experienced some acting success and was excited about his casting in an upcoming production of *Guys and Dolls*. I liked his spirit. He hadn't done anything special, except to make me feel good about my visit.

I'm on the final leg home. As we navigate the darkened skies, I'm watching a curly haired, blue-eyed two-and-a-half-year-old across the aisle and in front of me. This vibrant little thing hasn't yet realized it's night time. She sings. She laughs. She turns around to hold her daddy's hand as her big eyes look into his and she says, "I love you, Daddy!" Then she commences softly to sing her A-B-C's song. Through the crack in the seats, I can see her mother smile, nod approval, and struggle to stay awake.

Who will this little girl grow up to be? Will she become a rigid, uptight, stressed-out, weary adult? Or will she become another Leonardo, Audrey, Beau, or Bill? This sweet little thing has a multitude of choices to make as she grows up. These choices will determine who we see in 20, 30, or 40 years. I only hope she looks to those who have made responsible choices as her models.

Imagine that you are the adult that little girl models her life after. What will the result be? Will she love her chosen career? Will she find ways to positively affect the lives of people she comes in contact with? Will she continue smiling and innocently enjoying the little blessings of life? Will she face life's challenges with gusto and anticipation?

I endorse William Jennings Bryant's belief that "Destiny is not a matter of chance; but a matter of choice. It is not a thing to be waited for. It is a thing to be achieved." You can control your destiny and perspective of life, your job, and the people you encounter. The choices you make today, tomorrow, and next week build on each other to create a lifestyle that ultimately determines who you become, what you do, and what you have.

We can choose to welcome each new day with interest and curiosity, and as a new adventure, a new experience. We can also choose to dread every waking minute. We can choose to see an opportunity in every situation we encounter—or a crisis waiting to happen. We can choose to smile—or scowl. We can choose to plant seeds of fear, doubt, and dislike—or we can sow seeds of faith, hope, and love. We can choose to see others' positive characteristics and find them interesting and enjoyable—or we can choose to identify their annoyances and avoid interaction. The choice menu is endless.

I've learned you can give people a position or a job, but you cannot give them the qualities to be successful. People must choose whether or not to develop their qualities. Nothing will have a greater influence on your future than your decision to develop or bypass the characteristics of success.

Learning to love your job starts with understanding that you have choices. You are who you are and where you are today because of the choices you've made. If you want things to change, you have to make better choices. If you want to be a model of happiness, fulfillment, and contentment, eliminate the destructive choices that block these positive results. Act, walk, talk, and conduct yourself as the model person you can become. The only way you're going to make a change is to infuse yourself with a sense of urgency that continually nudges you to follow through.

Choose today to be the type of person that little girl on the airplane would be excited to become.

*The common idea that success spoils people by making them vain, ego-tistical, and self-complacent is erroneous; on the contrary, it makes them, for the most part, humble, tolerant, and kind. Failure makes people bitter and cruel.*

SOMERSET
MAUGHAM

## THE MAKINGS
## OF SUCCESS

Success might just come around, but most often it is the result of focused and concentrated effort. Reflecting upon her years of public service, Margaret Thatcher suggested that "Success is having a flair for the things that you are doing. Knowing that is not enough, you have got to have hard work and a certain sense of purpose."

Tom Morris, in his book *True Success,* offers these guidelines for achieving success:

1. "A conception of what you want. This means a vision, goal or set of goals, 'powerfully imagined.'

2. "A confidence to see it through. Without it, you'll never overcome obstacles.

3. "A concentration on what it takes. Prepared and plan and do. 'The world has more participants, more catalysts, agents of change . . .'

4. "A consistency in what you do. Be stubborn and persistent—even after failure.

5. "A commitment of emotional energy. Emerson said, 'Nothing great was ever achieved without enthusiasm.'

6. "A character of high quality. Integrity inspires trust and gets people pulling for you.

7. "A capacity to enjoy the process. The journey should be fun as well as challenging."

*I couldn't wait for success—so I went ahead without it.*

JONATHAN WINTERS

As you can plainly see, there are no new-fangled success secrets. The principles, process, and disciplines of success have been around since the beginning of time. The real issue here is that we cannot enjoy the benefits of success without the investment of sacrifice. Those people who want to wake up successful need to wake up. It's not going to happen any other way. "Success, real success in any endeavor," says James Rouche, "demands more from an individual than most people are willing to offer—not more than they are capable of offering." In other words, none of the writings, principles, secrets, processes work . . . unless you do.

# BREAK NEW GROUND

*I knew a man who grabbed a cat by the tail
and learned forty percent more about cats
than the man who didn't.*

MARK TWAIN

## IT'S NOT
## THAT BAD!

I can speak with experiential authority on the subject of mistakes. Although I'm not an advocate for making dumb mistakes on purpose, I've undoubtedly learned what to do and what not to do by doing what didn't work. If you're making any moves toward your goals or attempting to do things you've never done before, mistakes have probably become a normal part of your repertoire.

Mistakes are good for you. Motivational speaker Les Brown reminds us, "In order to get where you don't know you can go, you have to make mistakes to find out what you don't know." I know mistakes can be embarrassing, painful, and time consuming, but they are also marvelous teachers. In fact, going too long without a classic goof-up might be a serious indication that you've stopped learning, squelched your curiosity, or have settled into a comfort zone. It means you're aiming far too low and passing up the opportunity to pursue new levels of performance. That's dangerous. In fact, any one of these factors is the most serious mistake of all.

*Every great mistake has a halfway moment, a split second when it can be recalled and perhaps remedied.*

PEARL S. BUCK

❀

Mistakes are learning tools, growing pains, and character builders you encounter on the way to your goals. They are friends most people would rather avoid. Who wants to be hanging around with an acquaintance named "foul-up"? But this friend will help you find out how good you really are. As Nelson Boswell observed, "The difference between greatness and mediocrity is often how an individual views mistakes."

To help you keep your mistakes in perspective, I've gleaned some classic mishaps from newspapers, the Internet, and articles that friends have forwarded to me. Maybe yours won't seem so bad. Hopefully, you can learn something from their performances. If nothing else, learn to have a sense of humor. Goldie Hawn says, "Once you can laugh at your own weaknesses, you can move forward. Comedy breaks down walls. It opens up people. If you're good, you can fill up those openings with something positive. Maybe you can combat some of the ugliness in the world."

*New Women* magazine declared Linda Evans the winner of the "Most Embarrassing Moment Contest." Here was her submission: "It was Christmas Eve, and I was on my feet all day working behind the cosmetics counter. I decided I should find a place to sit for a moment. I spied a tall plastic trash can and plopped down, resting my feet on a cardboard box. I allowed my body to ease into the can. About that time a few customers came to the register to check out, but I couldn't get out of the trash can. I was stuck; I couldn't believe it. The customers came around the counter to help me—some pulled my arms while others held the can. Then my manager came to the counter, wanting to know what was going on. He said he was going to call the fire department, who blasted in with sirens and lights. My hips had created a vacuum, so they had to cut me out of the trash can with a giant pair of scissors."

I guess you could say she got "canned" without being fired. I'm sure Linda would be the first one to admit that her mistake got her derriere in a jam.

How would you like to be Janice? She spent nearly her whole vacation sunbathing on the roof of her hotel. She wore a two-piece bathing suit the first few days, but always removed her glasses to ensure an even facial tan.

After several days she decided no one could see her way up there, so she slipped out of her suit to get a full body tan. She'd just gotten comfortable when she heard someone running up the outside stairs of the hotel. She was lying on her stomach, so she just pulled a towel over her bottom.

"Excuse me, miss," said the out-of-breath, sweating hotel manager. "The hotel doesn't mind you sunbathing on the roof, but we would appreciate you putting your suit back on."

"I'm sorry if I've violated some rule," Janice replied.

"It's not that," the manager calmly replied. "You're lying on the dining room skylight."

*Oops!*

The pastor of a small church prided himself on being sensitive to the needs of his parishioners. Moments before the Sunday morning service, he overheard a man complain about back pain. His wife quickly explained that Jack was recovering from surgery.

During the morning prayer, the pastor thought of Jack and prayed that he might recover from surgery and be "restored to full function." Chuckles scattered throughout the church.

Jack's surgery was a vasectomy. Even good intentions can turn into innocent mistakes.

Joe Lomusio recorded this embarrassing moment in his book *If I Should Die Before I Live.* A tourist was standing in line to buy an ice cream cone at a Thrifty Drug store in Beverly Hills. To her utter shock and amazement, who should walk in and stand right behind her but Paul Newman! Well, the lady, even though she was rattled, was determined to maintain her composure. She purchased her ice cream cone, turned confidently, and exited the store.

However, to her horror, she realized that she had left the counter without her ice cream cone! She waited a few minutes until she felt all was clear, and then went back into the store to claim her cone. As she approached the counter, the cone was not in the little circular receptacle, and for a moment she stood there pondering what might have happened to it. Then she felt a polite tap on her shoulder and, turning was confronted by—you guessed it—Paul Newman. The famous actor then told the lady that if she was looking for her ice cream cone, she had put it into her purse.

Copley High School was leading Wadsworth by only two points in a crucial basketball game. A Copley fan used a defensive strategy not in the playbook. Just as a Wadsworth player was about to throw an inbound pass, a 16-year-old Copley student pulled the player's shorts down to his knees. It was a classic example of "being caught with your pants down."

Wadsworth coach John Martin said, "It was a critical stage of the game, and it was a must-win for our team. Can you imagine what kind of concentration our kid had after he was exposed?"

We can only imagine! Of course, the student defensive player didn't fare so well either. After being charged with disrupting a lawful meeting and disorderly conduct, the boy was suspended from school for an unspecified number of days and banned from extracurricular activities.

Picture this one. A man decided to take advantage of his wife being away to paint the bathroom toilet seat. After he finished, he headed for the refrigerator to reward himself with a cold drink.

His wife came home sooner than expected and headed straight for the bathroom. She sat down and got the toilet seat stuck to her rear. Of course she got upset and panicked. She shouted to her husband to help. He immediately put an overcoat over her to cover the toilet seat and headed for the doctor.

Parading into the doctor's office, the husband lifted the coat to reveal the predicament. He looked at the doctor and asked, "Have you ever seen anything like this before?"

"Well, yes," the doctor replied. "But never framed."

The next time you're tempted to respond to your mistakes by organizing a self-pity party, reflect on the clumsy, ridiculous and self-deprecating boo-boo's experienced by others. Your slip-ups and bumbling acts might not seem so bad. At any rate, Charles Handy suggests, "It's not the mistake that hurts us, it's the grace we employ owning up to it that counts."

"Nobody makes mistakes on purpose," says Leo Burnett, founder of the advertising agency Leo Burnett, Inc. "When you do make a mistake, I urge that you shouldn't let it gnaw at you, but should get it out into the open quickly so it can be dealt with. And you'll sleep better, too."

## MOVE THROUGH
## YOUR FEARS

*People are never more insecure than when they become obsessed with their fears at the expense of their dreams.*

NORMAN COUSINS

❀

According to a *Chicago Tribune* article entitled "Sign of the Times," police sharpshooters surrounded a car in Rochester, New York. In the back seat of the car was a man armed with a rifle. The police attempted to negotiate with the man but he refused to respond. The police patiently watched and waited until finally becoming suspicious. They made a surprising discovery: The armed man in the back seat was a mannequin.

When the owner of the car was found, he told the authorities he kept the mannequin in his car for protection. "You've got to do this," he said. "With the car-jackings, it helps if it looks like you've got a passenger."

We undoubtedly live in an age of fear. Horace Fletcher said, "Fear is an acid which is pumped into one's atmosphere. It causes mental, moral, and spiritual asphyxiation, and sometimes death; death to energy and all growth." Fear imprisons people. Fear keeps us from moving beyond where we are and from achieving our potential.

"Fear, to a degree," says Zig Ziglar, "makes procrastinators and cowards of us all." We all tend to possess mannequins intended to protect us from our fears.

Mannequins come in the form of low expectations, avoidance of risk, removal from potential conflict, shying away from new responsibilities, denying the reality of change or placing "do not touch" barriers around ourselves. These fear-protecting mannequins cause us to settle for far less than we are capable of and keep us from experiencing the fullness of life. As Edmund Burke said, "No passion so effectively robs the mind of all its powers of acting and reasoning as fear."

Swiss psychiatrist Paul Tournier, agreed: "All of us have reservoirs of our full potential, vast areas of great satisfaction, but the road that leads to those reservoirs is guarded by the dragon of fear."

This powerful life-stripping, adventure-robbing barrier is inside you. It's not the world . . . it's not your circumstances . . . it's not your job . . . it's not your past or the people in the present. It's the fear in you. The bad news is that fear sticks with us even when there is no real, concrete, or visible reason.

The good news is: Fear is learned and therefore can be unlearned. "Most fear is routed in ignorance," says Brian Tracy. "The more knowledge or skill you have in any area, the less fear it holds." It takes courage to overcome this fear-producing ignorance, but Karl A. Menninger reminded us that "Fears are educated into us and can, if we wish, be educated out."

The first and most difficult step in overcoming fear is courageous action. Professional boxing manager Cus D'Amato suggested, "The hero and the coward both feel exactly the same fear, only the hero confronts his fear and converts it to power." Everyone experiences fear one way or another. Only the victor makes an informed plunge forward.

In 1958 Woody Allen enjoyed a lucrative career as a comedy writer for television. He stayed behind the scenes because his biggest fear was appearing in front of an audience. Besides, the $75 a week stand-up comics were earning was only a token of the $1,700 he was earning doing the writing. Yet, Allen followed the urge to stretch beyond what he was doing. He got physically sick before every performance. He was applauded, booed, jeered, and cheered, but those who knew comedy revered him as a natural talent. "Talent is nothing," said Allen. "You're born with talent in the same way that basketball players are born tall. What really counts is courage. Do you have the courage to use the talent with which you were born?"

The great composer Ludwig van Beethoven lived much of his life fearing the possibility of deafness. How could anyone create a musical masterpiece without the benefit of hearing?

When that which he feared the most besieged him, Beethoven became frantic with anxiety. He consulted the specialists of his day and attempted every suggested remedy. Nothing worked.

Beethoven soon found himself living in a world of total quietness. He mustered the courage to move through his fear and the reality of deafness to write some of his finest musical masterpieces. The deafness shut out all distractions and the melodies flowed like never before. That which he had feared became a great asset.

Many people discover when coming face to face with their fear that their *fear* of fear was the only real fear. As Logan

Pearsall Smith put it, "What is more mortifying than to feel you have missed the plum for want of courage to shake the tree?" Fear possesses the powerful ability to hold us back, keep our talents in check, and cause us to miss life's fruit.

I would, in no way, want to give you the impression that fear can be mastered once and for all. Each time an event arises that surfaces your fear, you'll have to battle self-talk, imagination, expectations, and the memory of past experiences. Mentally work through the worst that could happen and the best possible thing that could happen if you were successful. Be realistic and, if at all possible, move forward. Fear is not overcome by merely thinking positive. By being realistic, a potentially overwhelming situation can be challenging, yet possible.

Action will reduce anxiety and tension, resulting in increased confidence and control.

"I believe that anyone can conquer fear," encouraged Eleanor Roosevelt, "by doing the things he fears to do, provided he keeps doing them until he gets a record of successful experiences behind him."

Realize that fear causes you to seek a comfort zone that holds you back from all that life has in store for you. Action propels you past these limitations toward the attainment of your goals and dreams. Move through your fears toward the realization of what you want and act as if it were impossible to fail.

*What success really means is looking failure in the face and tossing the dice anyway. You may be the only person who ever knows how the dice come up, but in that knowledge you have something that millions of people will never have— because they were afraid to try.*

*WRITER'S DIGEST*

❋

# BE A TEAM
# PLAYER

❋

*People are playing different instruments with different parts, but when they perform together from the same musical score, they produce beautiful music. They produce value.*

C. WILLIAM POLLARD
*The Soul of the Firm*

## BECOME A
## TRUST BUILDER

D
o you trust the people you work with? Do they trust you? The answers to these two questions will reveal volumes about the quality of your work environment. J. W. Driscoll said, "Trust has been shown to be the most significant predictor of individuals' satisfaction with their organization."

Trust between co-workers isn't just a nicety; trust is a mandatory ingredient for relationships to grow. "Without trust, there can be no cooperation between people, teams, departments, divisions," wrote quality expert Edwards Deming. "Without trust, each component will protect its own immediate interests to its own long-term detriment, and to the detriment of the entire system." Consider that advice from a person who helped countless companies pursue their optimum performance. Deming's experience revealed the universal importance of trust to achieve quality, innovation, service, and productivity.

*You can learn good manners to deal with people, but you can't learn to trust people. And you must trust to be comfortable with them.*

PETER
DRUCKER

❋

Low-trust environments struggle with rampant turn-over, absenteeism, unresolved conflict, low morale, dissatisfied customers, and a direct negative affect on the bottom line. In low-trust environments, people tell you what you want to hear. There is apathy, backbiting, and disloyalty. Defensiveness, territorialism, and an unwillingness to take responsibility for mistakes are commonplace. People live in fear and suspicion. The ramifications are endless, inevitable, and costly.

*Webster's* defines trust as "assured reliance on the character, ability, strength or trust of someone or something." In other words, trust means to have faith in, or to believe in, someone or something. Although we are generally a trusting generation, we are at a profound stage in history. Distrust and skepticism are subtly replacing belief and talent.

Bill Kynes wrote in *A Hope That Will Not Disappoint:*

"We thought we could trust the military,
　　but then came Vietnam;
"We thought we could trust the politicians,
　　but then came Watergate;
"We thought we could trust the engineers,
　　but then came the *Challenger* disaster;

"We thought we could trust our broker,
> but then came Black Monday;
"We thought we could trust the preachers,
> but then came PTL and Jimmy Swaggart.
"So who can I trust?"

You can no doubt add to the list reasons from recent events that discourage you from trusting.

"Trust is a calculated risk made with one's eyes open to the possibilities of failure," says Robert Levering, "but it is extended with the expectation of success."

This important organizational and relationship quality can be illustrated by the arrangement made between the shark and pilot fish. Sharks are renown for their indiscriminate palates and will enjoy a meal of almost any ocean dweller—that is, except the pilot fish. Instead, sharks extend an invitation for the pilot fish to join them for lunch; then, the smaller fish act as an automatic toothpick, eating the leftover food lodged between the sharks' teeth. It is a collaborative relationship; the shark gets clean teeth and better dental check-ups while the pilot fish gets nourished. Each fish is satisfied when the encounter is over.

Levering said trust is first of all a calculated risk. Second, it is extended with the expectation of success. So it is with the shark and pilot fish. First, the pilot fish trust the shark will not eat them and each fish knows that if it cooperates, their needs will be met.

I've hired hundreds of people in the past 25 years and have subscribed to one cardinal rule: Believe in and trust people until they prove themselves untrustworthy. In other words, trust begins with me, with my willingness to un-conditionally trust other people. This goes against the common grain to wait for people to prove themselves before you trust them. Trust will breed trust. Mistrust breeds mistrust. The surest way to help people prove themselves trustworthy is to trust them.

In his little book *Illustrations of Bible Truth,* H.A. Ironside pointed out the foolishness of judging others. He related an incident in the life of a man called Bishop Potter. "He was sailing for Europe on one of the great transatlantic ocean liners. When he went on board, he found that another passenger was to share the cabin with him. After going to see the accommodations, he came up to the purser's desk and inquired if he could leave his gold watch and other valuables in the ship's safe. He explained that ordinarily he never availed himself of that privilege, but he had been to his cabin and had met the man who was to occupy the other berth. Judging from his appearance, he was afraid that he might not be a very trustworthy person. The purser accepted the responsibility for the valuables and remarked, 'It's all right, Bishop, I'll be very glad to take care of them for you. The other man has been up here and left his for the same reason.'" Trust is a risk game and the person who antes up first will ultimately be a winner.

You can help build an environment of trust with others. Incorporate the following seven principles in your daily activities.

**1. Listen to people.** Attempt to understand their feelings, perspectives, and experiences. Always keep sensitive and private information confidential. Seek out others' ideas. We trust people who make a sincere attempt to understand who we are and what we are about.

**2. Be there for others.** When we make time for people, recognize their effort, celebrate their accomplishments, and value their opinions, a trust bond develops. Look for the unique talents and abilities in those you work with and tell them what you see. Don't spend excessive time on your own agenda or focused on just your personal welfare.

**3. Keep integrity intact.** Demonstrate through your actions that people can unquestionably believe what you say, know you will keep your promises, and can be assured you will be open with them. In other words, walk the talk. Be sure your attitudes and actions are consistent with your words. This is probably the most powerful method for obtaining people's trust.

**4. Refrain from gossip and feeding the grapevine.** Untruths, exaggeration, and backbiting quickly suffocate trust. Get the facts. Deal with reality rather than hearsay. The truth isn't always easy to deal with, but healing the wounds caused by misinformation is always painful. Nurture a culture of straightforward, open, and honest communication.

**5. Respect other people's values.** Diversity is a fact of life. You can't ignore it. Although you may not agree or endorse someone else's lifestyle, learn to respect his or her position. When you know and appreciate what others believe, a candid relationship can be achieved. Close-minded people rarely build open relationships.

**6. Care about people.** This seems so simple, yet we tend to get so caught up in the busyness of doing and meeting demands that people's needs often take a back seat. The payoff for taking the time to really care about someone else's personal welfare is significant. Help others achieve their goals and maintain their self-esteem. Thoughtfulness, respect, kindness, and a belief in people will breed success and trust.

**7. Mend broken fences.** Be willing to admit mistakes. Ask forgiveness. Restore peace where conflict has caused tension. Unhealed wounds will fester and infect relationships. Resist pointing an accusing finger when things go wrong. Take personal responsibility. Make amends.

Like all other relationship components, there is no magic formula for making trust suddenly appear. Trust isn't something we give attention to from nine to five; it requires a way of life that consistently displays, at minimum, the seven core principles for building trust. It takes an incredible commitment to develop the persistence, the patience, and the discipline to hold a relationship together for the long haul. Trust lies at the heart of this endeavor and consistency is the path that leads you there.

*The best proof of love is trust.*
JOYCE BROTHERS

❊

## WE ARE
## THE TEAM

O ne of the often overlooked benefits and responsibilities of teamwork is how we make others look.
Dynamic teams are composed of people who tend
to possess a genuine desire to make the team look good by
their performance. When team members fail to grasp this
concept and not live up to their end of the deal, it reflects on
the image of the entire team. Let me show you what I mean.

A 3-1/2 hour layover at Chicago O'Hare on a sunny and
warm April Sunday afternoon is not on my top ten list of
"Most Desirable Things to Do!" Unboarding the plane, my
mind raced through ideas that would help me endure this
boring necessity. Being a people-watcher holds my attention
for a short time and then I'm looking for other avenues to
pass time.

Bookstores always draw my attention and often tap my
wallet. I found one a short distance from my departure gate
and decided to invest some time browsing the latest titles,

reading a few pages here and there, and generally "sampling" the merchandise. Convinced an hour had passed, I reentered the corridor and glanced at my watch. It stopped running. No wait, the second hand was moving. Only 12 minutes had elapsed. Now what?

The smell of freshly brewed gourmet coffee is a second temptation to which I often succumb. Ordering the biggest cup they offered and purchasing an equally tempting pastry, I decided to make my way to the seating area at the gate and wait out my layover.

As I entered the end of the terminal on "B" concourse, my eyes fell on a young man sitting in a wheelchair with a heavy coat on, zipped up to his neck. His head was cocked back, eyes were tightly closed, and it was evident he was soundly sleeping.

"How sad," I thought to myself. "Here is a young man who could be making something of himself. Instead, he's homeless and comes to the airport to sleep off his nightly activities."

I continued reading a book I started earlier on the trip, and periodically glanced over at the limp body that hadn't moved since I sat down.

"What could he be dreaming about? Where will he go when he finally awakens? What awaits him in his day-to-day surroundings?"

"Hey, Jimmy!" a powerful voice blared behind me.

The young man was startled awake.

"You on break?"

"No," he responded groggily. "Can't you see I'm working?"

"Then I need you to push this lady to gate B-2. She has a plane to catch in 15 minutes."

"Ah, man," he responded as he slowly removed his heavy coat and threw it over the bench next to him.

To my surprise, he was dressed in the uniform of the airlines I was flying with. I had to smile. Here I was judging and stereotyping without having the facts. The sad thing is, the facts were as bad as my misguided conclusions. What I had just witnessed had to be a fluke.

To say he was excited about performing his duties would be a drastic overstatement. His eyes were open but his mind hadn't told his feet to start functioning. He shuffled behind the wheelchair, slowly pushing his elderly customer to her destination.

I stayed glued to my seat to observe how this situation would unfold. Would the lady in her wheelchair make her flight? Would Jimmy return to resume his nap? How would the airline employees respond?

Upon Jimmy's return to the area (which took place as slowly as he had exited), a few cohorts arrived to visit. "Gee, I hate it when the old bag wakes me up," he told his friends. "I was really enjoying myself. What time is it anyway?" When the conversation with his buddies ended, he put his coat back on, zipped it up, and resumed his sleeping position.

I couldn't believe my ears. This was no homeless, destitute, unwanted person. He was an airline employee bothered by the command to wake up and do his job. When I left the area an hour later, his mouth was hanging wide open as he periodically engaged in a gross sounding cough/snore. Not one employee questioned his status as they paraded by. He lived and worked (I use the term loosely) in his own world.

I spent that flight reflecting on how Jimmy's behavior clouded my perceptions of the entire airline. Not one of Jimmy's teammates said anything to him about his lethargic, unprofessional, lazy behavior. I wondered if they realized the

*The main ingredient of stardom is the rest of the team.*

JOHN WOODEN

❀

impression he gave to the rest of the airline employees. Did they really want to be associated with such incompetence?

The more I thought, the more infuriated I became. But wait a minute. How many times are we guilty of excusing the performance of people on our teams with such justification as "That's just the way Jimmy is." "Mary has always been negative." "Pete just isn't a team player." "Sally has never had much get up and go."

Coach John Wooden believed that if everyone does not accept his or her role and play it to the best of his or her ability, "the group as a whole is going to suffer." Through our consistent, active participation, we can help our team develop a winning reputation.

PRACTICE THE
ART OF ENCOURAGEMENT

Basketball great Michael Jordan was asked by columnist Bob Greene why he wanted his father to be in the stands during a basketball game. Jordan replied, "When he's there, I know I have at least one fan." No matter how strong, self-confident, popular, or competent you are, feeling the support of a loyal fan can be just the encouragement you need to make it through a new challenge, difficult project, or even a tedious task.

Likewise, you can be that loyal fan for other people. Oftentimes people become so concerned about not being able to do great things for someone else that they neglect to do the little things that can be equally as meaningful and effective. One of those "little things" you can do is to provide encouragement. Somebody once said, "Encouragement is the fuel for tomorrow." Encouragement rewards people for who they are and gives them hope in doing all they can do and becoming all they can be.

*Flatter me, and I may not believe you. Criticize me, and I may like you. Ignore me, and I may not forgive you. Encourage me, and I will not forget you.*
WILLIAM ARTHUR WARD

Many years ago, an interesting experiment was conducted to measure people's ability to endure pain. Psychologists were interested in measuring how long a barefoot person could stand in a bucket of ice water. (Anyone who has ever had a severely sprained ankle understands the discomfort in this exercise.) Anyway, experiment results showed that one factor significantly affected some people's ability to endure the pain twice as long as others. The common factor was encouragement. Those people who had someone nearby giving support and encouragement were able to endure the pain much longer than those who were left to themselves.

We all know how the smallest gesture, kind comment, genuine word of encouragement, quick compliment, or praise for a job well done can make a lasting difference in someone's life. Yet, we don't always take the time to let people know our heartfelt thoughts and give them a small gift of happiness.

Find a 3 x 5 note card. Think about one person you work with who could benefit from a personal message that would make him or her feel good about him- or herself. Choose whatever quality, talent, action that you have observed in that person's life. What is it about that person that you appreciate? Why are you glad to have the privilege of working with this person? What has this person done this week to make you smile, lift a load, or add value to the team?

Make your message personal. Use the person's first name. Write your message of encouragement in the first person and express how you feel about the person. Be as specific as you can. Orison Swett Marden believed, "There is no investment you can make which will pay you so well as the effort to scatter sunshine and good cheer through your establishment." That's exactly what this little exercise is intended to do.

Help people believe in themselves. Build their confidence and self-esteem. Make a concentrated effort to see that people feel important and appreciated. Celebrate and get excited about others' successes. Be a cheerleader. Point out strengths and contributions. Bring a ray of sunshine with you to work everyday and scatter it liberally wherever you go.

You can be a hero in your organization by becoming a picker-upper person. Make it a way of life rather than a periodic or one-time event.

*We all need encouragement. We can live without it just as a young tree can live without fertilizer, but unless we receive that warm nurturing, we never reach our full potential, and like the tree left to itself, we seldom bear fruit.*

FLORENCE
LITTAUER

❋

# LOOSEN UP...
# LIGHTEN UP...
# HAVE FUN!

❋

*A fun working environment is much more
productive than a routine environment.
People who enjoy their work will come up
with more ideas. The fun is contagious.*

ROGER VON OECH

## AN ENTERTAINING
## FLIGHT ATTENDANT

G ood morning, ladies and gentlemen! Welcome aboard United Airlines flight 548, direct from Palm Springs to Chicago."

Wait a minute! My mind starts racing. I know it's early in the morning, 6:50 A.M. to be exact, but I was sure this flight went to Denver.

"Now that I got your attention," the voice continues, "my name is Annamarie and I'll be your first flight attendant today. Actually, we will be en route to Denver so if you were not planning to go there, now would be a good time to get off the plane.

"Safety is important to us so please take out the safety card in the pocket in front of you and acquaint yourself with the procedures. Come on, everybody, take out those brochures and wave them in the air! (70% of the passengers chuckle and do as they are told; 20% aren't awake yet; and the other 10% are sourpusses) Thank you. Thank you.

*I have always been able to gain my living without doing any work. I enjoyed the writing of books and magazine matter; it was merely billiards to me.*

MARK TWAIN

❋

"In the event that we mistakenly land in a body of water, a decision must be made. You can either pray and swim like crazy, or use your seat as a flotation device.

"We will be serving breakfast in flight this morning. On the menu I have eggs benedict and fruit crepes . . . not really, but they sound good to me. However, the flight attendants will be offering your choice of an omelet or cold cereal."

William Faulkner once lamented that "The saddest thing in life is that the only thing we can do for eight hours a day, day after day, is work. We can't eat for eight hours a day, or drink for eight hours a day, or make love for eight hours a day. All that we can do for that long a period," he said, "is work, which is the reason man makes himself and everybody so miserable and unhappy."

I'm thankful the flight attendant on flight 548 didn't possess Faulkner's attitude about work. It was evident she enjoyed what she did. Her entertaining approach to a normally routine, boring takeoff procedure endeared her to the passengers. Think of the innumerable benefits people would experience were they to add this positive approach to their normal routine.

John Maxwell summed it up quite well when he said, "I choose to have fun. Fun creates enjoyment. Enjoyment invites participation. Participation focuses attention. Attention expands awareness. Awareness promotes insight. Insight generates knowledge. Knowledge facilitates action. Action yields results."

PUT YOUR WORK
IN PERSPECTIVE

*The master in
the art of living
makes little
distinction
between his
work and his
play, his labor
and his
leisure . . .
He hardly
knows which is
which.*

JAMES A.
MICHENER

❋

I'm almost embarrassed to admit it, but about once a year I find myself rewatching and enjoying The *Mighty Ducks,* the highly successful Disney movie about a youth hockey team that rises from anonymity to celebrity.

The movie opens with a flashback scene of a demanding, tough, overbearing hockey coach convincing a young player, Gordon Bombay, to attempt a crucial penalty shot. "If you miss this shot," he says, "you'll let me down and you'll let your team down!" The frightened boy manipulates the puck, takes his best shot, and barely misses the goal. The burden of that loss and the shame of letting his team down dramatically affects Gordon Bombay for years to come.

Bombay unexpectedly becomes the coach of a group of struggling youth called the District Five Ducks. They know they are bad and Bombay reinforces all the bad they believe about themselves. He berates them, insults them, teaches them to cheat, and continually pressures them to meet unrealistic expectations. He becomes the coach he had as a youth . . . and hates it.

Gordon Bombay gradually learns that having fun on the ice is a worthy goal of any player or coach. The *Mighty Ducks* learn to believe in themselves, support each other, refine their skills, and have fun playing hockey. Bombay works hard to nurture the enjoyment of the game in his young skaters, and in the closing chapter of the movie, he takes his team of Ducks into a championship playoff game. The opposing top-rated team is tough, big, mean, and coached by none other than his old coach, Jack Riley.

Riley's strategy hasn't changed a bit. He berates. He insults. He threatens. Bombay has endorsed a different approach. "More fun! More fun!" the team chants in the huddle with Bombay leading the cheer.

The Hawks and the Ducks skate to a 4–4 tie as the final gun sounds. But one of the Hawks has fouled a Duck player, giving the Ducks a penalty shot—one chance to win the championship.

Coach Bombay chooses Charlie Conway to take the final shot. Bombay's touching dialog with Charlie is the exact opposite of the conversation in the opening scene of the movie. "You may make it, you may not," Coach Bombay tells Charlie. "But that doesn't matter. What matters is that we're here. Look around. Who'd ever have thought we would make it this far? Take your best shot. I believe in you, Charlie, win or lose."

Charlie grins, accepts the challenge, and sends the puck into the opponent's goal. The underdog Ducks win the championship.

I like this movie a lot because it portrays the type of environment and message needed in our organizations and personal careers. Willie Stargell, the retired baseball star, once remarked that at the start of a ballgame, you never hear an umpire yelling "Work ball." Of course not. They always yell "Play ball!" Let me push this a bit further. I wonder what would happen if the people you work with started every work day reminding themselves "I get to play today." Work should be a fun, marvelous, exciting game.

Instead, I run into people in a variety of careers who struggle with:

- Low self-esteem
- Feeling overwhelmed by job and people demands
- Uncertainty about their future

- Feelings of powerlessness to make things better
- Busyness without results
- A lack of meaning and satisfaction in their work
- Routine, monotony, and boredom

People say they don't have time to have fun anymore, or they can't wait until the weekend so they can live again. Other people view their work as an interruption between free hours. Pressure, stress, and loss of control haunt still others. Edward L. Bernays reminds us, "Never permit a dichotomy to rule your life, a dichotomy in which you hate what you do so you can have pleasure in your spare time. Look for a situation in which your work will give you as much happiness as your spare time." What marvelous advice!

The *Mighty Ducks* movie tends to put things in perspective. Work is meant to be enjoyed. In fact, when you learn to relax, enjoy the hours, refine your skills, give your best, and nurture those around you, a refreshing attitude of satisfaction will evolve. Try it. See for yourself that the pressure cooker many of us work in can be relieved by the soothing efforts of others, and by taking responsibility for self-induced negative feelings and thoughts about what we do for a living.

*Love what
you're doing
and don't
retire... I
would rather
be a failure
at something
I love than
a success at
something I
hate.*

GEORGE
BURNS

"Work is a four-letter word," suggested Al Sacharov. "It's up to us to decide whether that four-letter word reads 'drag' or 'love.' Most work is a drag because it doesn't nourish our souls. The key is to trust your heart to move where your talents can flourish. This old world will really spin when work becomes a joyous expression of the soul."

## REFILLS ARE
## FREE

The short 36 minute flight wasn't enough time for the flight attendants to serve beverages. Considering the early morning hour, most of us quickly made our way to the nearest airport coffee shop as soon as we exited the plane.

I took my place in line behind the other 20 caffeine-deprived travelers. We were all entertained watching and listening to the server behind the counter. She was singing along with the oldies music on the radio, dancing, taking orders, working the cash register, flipping cups (before filling), and serving the coffee and goodies. If she didn't thoroughly enjoy her job, someone should nominate her for an Emmy award-winning performance.

As I approached the counter to place my order, she continued to entertain the customers with her perky personality. The man behind me jokingly commented, "You've got to get over this depression."

*We can determine our optimum speed of living by trying various speeds and finding out which one is most agreeable.*

HANS SELYE

Misunderstanding his attempt at humor and unable to clearly hear what he said, she quickly replied, "Pressure? What pressure? I don't feel any pressure!"

I seemed to enjoy that morning's coffee a bit more than usual as I reflected on the events that had just taken place at the coffee bar. Here was a barista who had clearly decided her optimum speed of living. Because she was energetic, gregarious, fun-loving, and friendly at 7:00 A.M., some people were suspicious of her behavior. How could anyone move at that pace this early and enjoy what she was doing?

I'm finding it increasingly curious how moving slow, being sarcastic and negative, disliking your job, and dragging your way through life is considered normal. But show a little positive emotion, smile, and enjoy the day, and you're a candidate for being labeled unrealistic.

The truth is, we each choose our optimum speed and nature of living. Unfortunately, some people have quit trying anything but the rut to which they are accustomed. That's their choice. It's unfortunate, but until they decide to put a little zip in their step, they'll continue to reap mediocre results.

I like being with people who like life. I enjoy the company of friends who enjoy their work. I choose to spend time with people who choose to make the most of every moment they're breathing. Hang around these kinds of people and they will help you continually adjust and improve your speed of living.

I think I'll go back for a refill. I could use a little inspiration.

*One of the symptoms of an approaching nervous break- down is the belief that one's work is terribly important.*

BERTRAND RUSSELL

❁

## HAVE A LITTLE
## FUN

*He who does
not get fun
and enjoyment
out of every
day . . . needs
to reorganize
his life.*

GEORGE
MATTHEW
ADAMS

A few years ago, my wife gave me a gift certificate on Valentine's Day for a one-hour massage. I've never indulged the services of a massage therapist but it sounded like a fun experience so I immediately called for an appointment.

Let me preface the remainder of this story with a bit of insight about my personality. I enjoy a periodic practical joke that creates a bit of humor or good clean fun. I normally reserve such antics for people I know well, but this day, a rare opportunity surfaced I just couldn't resist.

The therapist greeted me in her lobby and, after a bit of small talk, she asked what type of massage I preferred. I weighed the options and decided on deep muscle therapy. The therapist was cordial and professional as she led me into the room and turned on some "mood" music, assembled her lotions and lit a few scented candles. Then it happened.

"Glenn, I'm going to leave the room for a few minutes," she said. "Would you please disrobe down to your underwear."

I mustered a serious expression and replied, "I don't wear underwear!"

The laughter that followed, once she realized I was only kidding, probably stimulated more endorphins than the massage that followed.

I feel sorry for people whose lives are so regimented that they are unable to produce, or at least enjoy, periodic doses of fun. I realize fun isn't for everyone. It's only for people who want to enjoy life and feel alive. For all others, there is tension, stress, ulcers, headaches, and boredom. The decision on which path to take sounds like a no-brainer to me.

Charlie Chaplin said, "If you've got something funny to do, you don't have to be funny to do it." You don't have to change your personality to have fun. It does require you to look for the ridiculous, slightly humorous, absurd, entertaining events in everyday life. Having fun isn't something you necessarily learn; it is a perspective on life that you give yourself permission to enjoy.

*A light heart lives long.*
WILLIAM
SHAKESPEARE

❀

As I drove through a small town in southern Iowa, I noticed a fun-loving radiator repair shop that posted this motto on its sign: "The best place in town to take a leak." I was equally impressed with some plumbers who approached their business with a bit of levity. Painted across the side of their van was this saying: "In our business, a fush beats a full house." That's the kind of plumber I want doing my work. Finally, a muffler shop in a small town in Nebraska made this attempt at fun: "No appointment necessary. We'll hear you coming." The people responsible for these signs have given themselves permission to express a perspective on life that produces a little fun.

Consider again the words of George Matthew Adams: "He who does not get fun and enjoyment out of every day . . . needs to reorganize his life." Is it time for you to do a little reorganizing?

Glenn Van Ekeren is the Executive Vice President for Vetter Health Services in Omaha, Nebraska, a company committed to providing "dignity in life" for the elderly. He is a frequent speaker on principles for maximizing people and organizational potential. He is the author of a number of books including 12 Simple Secrets of Happiness (Prentice Hall Press, 2000), Speaker's Sourcebook I and II, and is a featured author in several Chicken Soup Books.

For further information about Glenn Van Ekeren's seminars and other products, contact:

Glenn Van Ekeren
21134 Arbor Court
Elkhorn, Nebraska 68022
402-289-4523